BARRON'S

Painless Junior

Grammar

Marciann McClarnon, M.S.

Donna Christina Oliverio, M.S.
Contributing Editor

BARRON'S

Dedication

This book is dedicated to Devin, Lauren, and Kelsey—my
very first and my most favorite students.

All inquiries should be addressed to:
Barron's Educational Series, Inc.
250 Wireless Boulevard
Hauppauge, New York 11788
www.barronseduc.com

Library of Congress Catalog Card No.: 2006032248
ISBN-13: 978-0-7641-3561-3
ISBN-10: 0-7641-3561-9

Library of Congress Cataloging-in-Publication Data

McClarnon, Marciann.
   Painless junior grammar / Marciann McClarnon.
      p.   cm.
   Includes index.
   ISBN-13: 978-0-7641-3561-3
   ISBN-10: 0-7641-3561-9
   1. English language—Grammar—Juvenile literature. 2. English language—Usage—Juvenile
literature. 3. Language arts (Elementary)—Juvenile literature. I. Title
   LB1576.M277   2007
   372.61—dc22   2006032248

PRINTED IN THE UNITED STATES OF AMERICA
9 8 7 6 5 4 3 2 1

Contents

Introduction

Where would you go if you could visit anywhere in the world? For a lot of kids, the answer is a theme park. You have probably visited a theme park or at least seen one in the movies or on television.

The setting of *Painless Junior Grammar* is a magical theme park called Grammar World. So, in these pages, you will not only learn about the pieces of language and become a better speaker and writer, but you will also have more fun than a chipmunk with a berry. You will go on fast and furious rides, touch the tail of a beluga whale, pet furry and feathered friends, enjoy live shows, and be dazzled by the brightest fireworks!

This book invites you to get up close to many interesting characters. One of them is a kooky, but loveable, chicken named Shakespeare. He lives at Grammar World and will be your guide when you visit the theme park.

Shakespeare loves adventure. He has nerves of steel but a heart of gold. Last week, Shakespeare rode the mega-scary giant slide so many times that he wore a hole smack dab in the center of his favorite foam mat. In fact, he almost wore out the seat of his swimming trunks. (Yikes!) That didn't stop him. He just kept sliding until Grammar World closed for the evening.

All this talk about theme parks is making me think about roller coasters, musical carousels, rock climbing towers, go-carts, video arcades, safari adventures, and much more. I wonder what YOU are thinking or imagining.

Are you ready for some twisting and turning, whirling and twirling, wading and whooshing, splashing and swirling? If so, all you have to do is strap yourself in, turn the page, and hold on! How many thrills you seek and how wet you get is up to you!

ABOUT GRAMMAR WORLD

In *Chapter One*, the adorable animals that live at Grammar World greet you and help you learn about sentences. The painless news is that there are many interesting ways to put words together and still get your point across.

Chapter Two is about people, places, animals, things, and ideas—in other words, nouns. Adjectives are also defined and listed. Adjectives describe nouns and pronouns. Our language would be pretty dull without adjectives. It would be like popcorn with no salt or iced tea in Georgia without sugar. Yuck! Boring!

Chapter Three deals with verbs. You know about verbs. They add the action. Language would be frozen without them. Verbs are so important that without them there would be no sentences. They are the engines that power our language and make it go! Vrooom!

Verbs come in different shapes and sizes. Some are busy action verbs like *run*, *sneeze*, and *jump*. Some are linking verbs or verbs of being; they may not be busy action verbs, but they are important, too. Without them, you would cease existing because you could not "be." The most common linking verbs are *is, are, was, am,* and *were*. Helping verbs are the third category of verbs. They are words like *can, have,* and *will*. The sentence "I have given you enough cookies." just wouldn't sound right without the helping verb *have*.

Chapter Four focuses on prepositions, conjunctions, and interjections.

To identify a preposition, imagine a place such as a cave and think about where you are in relation to that place. For example, you could be *above* it, *beside* it, *in* it, or *under* it. Imagine also the movements you might make regarding the cave. You could, for example, go *around* the cave or *through* it.

Conjunctions are like glue or the sticky sap that comes out of trees in the spring. You get the idea. Conjunctions connect. They are words like *but, so*, and *and*. (That looks weird, but it's correct.)

Interjections make you jump as if you were stepping on hot beach sand. Wow! Gosh! Hurray! They get a strong feeling across and often do so in just one word.

Chapter Five is about mechanics, and I am not talking about someone who fixes your car when it breaks down. Mechanics includes punctuation and capitalization.

Punctuation marks are like the crossing guard at your school. They help direct or guide you. From commas to quotation marks and all the other punctuation marks in between, you'll be amazed by the number of punctuation marks that you as a writer can use. Just look at any computer keyboard and you'll see a collection of punctuation marks.

You already know that you should capitalize the proper names of people, places, and things, as well as the first word in a sentence. There are also other times when you should use uppercase letters. Check out Chapter Five to get the whole scoop.

Chapter Six gives you the opportunity to practice what you have learned throughout this book.

How do you improve a batting average or a tennis serve? How do you better your score on the football or soccer field? How do you bake a chewier brownie? You practice! That's also how you become a better grammar student. Chapter Six is just perfect for practicing how to practice. Does that make sense?

Icon Key

Lets Try It!
A quiz to practice
what you just learned.

Trick to Remember
Important hints that you
should keep in mind.

Careful!
Watch out for
possible problems.

Treasure Hunt
Find examples of
a certain topic

Treasure Chest
Examples of a certain topic

Wrapping It Up
A summary of key ideas

Hitting the Target
Practice of the chapter's
key ideas

Chapter I

Sentences—The Animals

SENTENCES

A sentence is like a train. The *words* are the cars that connect and work together.

Let's look at some examples of sentences and some nonsentences.

This is a sentence: *Our safari vehicle traveled over some bumpy roads.*

This is not a sentence: *traveled over some bumpy roads*

This is a sentence: *The animals that live at Grammar World love children.*

This is not a sentence: *The animals*

Now that you've read the examples above, can you describe in your own words what a sentence is?

A sentence is a group of words that expresses a complete thought.

Every sentence has two parts: a <u>subject</u> and a <u>predicate</u>.

- A subject tells who or what the sentence is about. The subject is a noun or pronoun.

- A predicate tells what the subject is or does. The verb is found in the predicate.

Let's take another look at our nonsentences.

traveled over some bumpy roads

This is not a sentence because the reader does not know WHO traveled over some bumpy roads. Was it Shakespeare, the students,

Abraham Lincoln, or some other person, animal, or object? The reader cannot answer the question because the subject of the sentence is missing.

The animals

This is not a sentence because the reader does not know WHAT. What are the animals or what are they doing or what did they do? Are the animals eating grass or did they greet the children? The reader has no clue because the predicate of the sentence is missing.

STATEMENTS AND QUESTIONS

- A declarative sentence makes a statement. It tells something about someone or something. It ends in a period.

   Tim cheered loudly when the lion jumped through the hoop.

- An interrogative sentence asks a question. It ends with a question mark.

   Why is Libby leaving before the tigers arrive?

Let's Try It!
Set #1

Which of these sentences are declarative and which are interrogative? The end punctuation mark will give you a clue.

1. Kelsey applauded as the ringmaster blew his whistle.
2. Why did Riley arrive so late?
3. Have you seen the white tiger act?

4. Tom wanted to sit by his best friend during the Animal Magic Show.

5. The rain poured on the cheering train riders.

6. Libby wanted to feed the monkeys.

7. When can we visit the petting zoo?

8. Where in the world is Shakespeare?

9. Once upon a time in a magical theme park not so far away, there was a jungle full of amazing animals.

10. Even after a long day at Grammar World, Tim did not want to leave.

Answers are on page 139.

COMMANDS AND EXCLAMATIONS

An imperative sentence asks or tells someone to do something. It is a request or command. It ends in a period or an exclamation point.

Watch out!

Please take your little sister to feed the giraffes.

An exclamatory sentence or exclamation expresses strong feeling. It ends with an exclamation point.

A tiger has escaped!

What a fantastic time we are having at Grammar World!

5

Let's Try It!
Set #2

Which of the following are commands and which are exclamations? (Don't let the end mark fool you.)

1. Meet me at the wooden roller coaster after lunch.
2. Watch out!
3. What a magical day!
4. Go to the middle of the park.
5. Grammar World is the best place to learn!
6. Take the Play Land express train.
7. Look out below!
8. Please help your sister find her heart necklace.
9. Come home before it gets dark.
10. Yes!

Answers are on page 139.

Type of sentence	What does it tell?	End mark
Statement or declarative sentence	Makes a statement	Period (.)
Question or interrogative sentence	Asks a question	Question mark (?)
Command or imperative sentence	Tells or asks someone to do something	Exclamation point (!) or period (.)
Exclamation or exclamatory sentence	Shows strong feeling	Exclamation point (!)

Trick to Remember

It is important to choose the correct end mark for your sentence because it tells readers how you are feeling. If you want to show strong feeling, use an exclamation point rather than a period. I mean it! I'm not kidding!

SUBJECTS AND PREDICATES

Like a train, a sentence needs certain parts to run properly. The sentence must be complete.

Every sentence has two parts: a *subject* and a *predicate*.

*   A *subject* tells who or what the sentence is about. The subject is a noun or a pronoun.

    <u>Alex</u> *fed the birds at the theme park.*

    <u>Kelsey</u> *rode the train ten times.*

*   A *predicate* tells what the subject is or does. The verb is found in the predicate.

    Alex <u>fed the birds at the theme park.</u>

    Kelsey <u>rode the train ten times.</u>

The subject and the predicate have to work together to make a sentence complete.

The subject is like the engine of a train. It runs the sentence and is usually found at the very front.

The complete subject is the **who** or **what** that is doing the verb **plus** all the descriptive words that go with it. Look at the following sentence.

The tall, purple clown performed in the dog show.

Who performed? The clown, of course. But this clown wasn't short and red. No, this one was tall and purple. The complete subject, then, is **the tall, purple clown**.

Let's look at a few more examples.

The long-necked tiger smiles when Shakespeare is around.

Complete subject: *The long-necked tiger*

The entire class wanted to learn more about endangered species.

Complete subject: *The entire class*

The predicate is like one of the cars in a train. It adds detail and information. The complete predicate is all the words that tell what the subject is or does.

All the students got the chance to feel the tail of a beluga whale.

Complete predicate: *got the chance to feel the tail of a beluga whale*

Grammar World is brimming with all your favorite animal buddies.

Complete predicate: *is brimming with all your favorite animal buddies.*

Trick to Remember

To figure out whether or not a *sentence* is complete, ask yourself two questions:

1. *Who or what is doing something?* (If you can answer this question, the sentence has a subject.)

2. *What is happening?* (If you can answer this question, the sentence has a predicate/verb.)

If you can answer both of these questions, your sentence is complete. Jump up and down and spin round and round. You are a grammarian (a grammar wiz)!

Complete Subject	Complete Predicate
The amazing animals	performed for the audience.
Molly and Casey	cheered for the lion tamer.
Adrianna	frowned when the show ended.

Let's Try It!
Set #3

Read each of the following sentences carefully. Put one line under the complete subject and two lines under the complete predicate.

1. The students in Mr. Larsen's class gave each other high five's when they won free tickets to see the dancing bear show.

2. Peter and Tyler played in the Grammar World All-Star Band.

3. The sun smiled on the playful children.

4. Molly fixed the stage for the performance.

5. Four kittens were born on Saturday.

6. Shakespeare sang the children's favorite song.

7. Tim and Todd played football at the dome.

8. Libby will ride the monorail to get to the other side of the park.

9. Black clouds filled the sky before the storm.

10. The third-graders won the contest at the water park.

Answers are on page 140.

Compound Subjects

One of the cool things about grammar is that it gives you a chance to play with words and language. Let's say, for example, that you've written the following two sentences:

Shakespeare ran with the children.

The teacher ran with the children.

After rereading your sentences, you decide to combine them as follows:

Shakespeare and the teacher ran with the children.

Grammar has a name for what you've just created. You've created a compound subject. You've taken the simple subject *Shakespeare* and the simple subject *the teacher*, combined them, and had them share the same predicate *ran*. Compound subjects can make your writing flow like a peaceful waterfall.

When two or more simple subjects have the same predicate, the sentence has a compound subject.

Let's look at some other examples of compound subjects.

The monkey stole the show.

Monkey = simple subject; *stole* = predicate

The peacock stole the show.

The monkey and the peacock stole the show.

Isabella rode the monorail.

Molly rode the monorail.

Isabella and Molly rode the monorail.

Let's Try It!
Set #4

Complete the following activity by doing what is asked.

Combine each group of two sentences (1 through 5) to make a sentence that has a compound subject. The first one has been done for you.

1. The bus driver was sunburned.

   Many of the children were sunburned.

   The bus driver and many of the children were sunburned.

2. Scott ate pizza for lunch.

   Lauren ate pizza for lunch.

   _____

3. Tim waited patiently for the afternoon parade.

Todd waited patiently for the afternoon parade.

_____

4. Ariel wore comfortable sneakers to Grammar World.

Sam wore comfortable sneakers to Grammar World.

_____

5. Lauren enjoyed a long nature walk.

Tracy enjoyed a long nature walk.

_____

Sentences 6 through 10 contain compound subjects.
Underline the compound subject in each sentence.

6. Shakespeare and the children saw an animal puppet show.

7. Dillan and Lindsay ate breakfast with their favorite characters.

8. Saturday and Sunday were the busiest days to visit the park.

9. Mr. Katz and Ms. Leon chaperoned the field trip.

10. All the children and their parents stopped for lemonade and honey-dipped pretzels.

Answers are on page 140.

COMPOUND PREDICATES

What do you think of these two sentences?

The lion danced.

The lion roared.

Shakespeare thinks that they're a good start, but he is always looking for ways to improve his writing. How can we make these sentences sound less choppy and more exciting? How about combining them?

The lion danced. + The lion roared. = The lion danced and roared.

Combining these sentences was as easy as riding the merry-go-round because each of them had the same subject, *the lion*. Do you think the combined sentence sounds better than the two separate ones? (Shakespeare does!)

In the sentence "The lion danced and roared," the subject (*lion*) has two predicates (*danced* and *roared*). When a subject has two or more predicates, the subject has a compound predicate.

In the following example, the first two sentences in the group have been combined to make a new sentence containing a compound predicate.

Shakespeare shooed away a bee that was ruffling his feathers.

Shakespeare patted himself on the back for his bee-chasing talents.

*Shakespeare **shooed** away a bee that was ruffling his feathers and **patted** himself on the back for his bee-chasing talents.*
(Shakespeare = subject; *shooed*, *patted* = compound predicate)

Let's Try It!

Set #5

Complete the following activity by doing what is asked.

Combine each group of two sentences (1 through 3) to make a sentence that has a compound predicate.

1. Alex licked his fingers after eating the tasty brownie.

    Alex washed his hands.

    _____

2. Peter strolled through the animal gallery at Grammar World.

    Peter admired the colorful posters and photographs.

    _____

3. The animals at Grammar World jump for joy when children arrive at the theme park.

    The animals at Grammar World feel down in the dumps when the children leave.

    _____

Sentences 4 through 8 contain compound predicates. Underline the compound predicate in each sentence.

4. The polite children picked up litter on the ground at Grammar World and threw it in a nearby trash can.

5. Shakespeare thanked the children for helping to keep the theme park clean and gave them cuddly stuffed teddy bears for their efforts.

6. The children were proud of themselves for what they had done and promised to always respect the environment.

7. Cory went to the art corner and made a poster about our environment and the precious animals that live in it.

8. Joe believes that Grammar World treats the animals that live there kindly and hopes that other theme parks and zoos do as well.

Answers are on page 141.

COMBINING SENTENCES

Two sentences can be joined by adding a conjunction. Conjunctions are connecting words like *and*, *or,* and *but*.

Two sentences:

> *Tyler ate cheese popcorn.*
>
> *Tyler ate chocolate peanuts.*

Joining sentences by adding a conjunction:

> *Tyler ate cheese popcorn and chocolate peanuts.*

Two sentences:

> *Peter will meet us in front of the peacock cage.*
>
> *Laura will be near the goats.*

Joining two sentences by adding a conjunction:

Peter will meet us in front of the peacock cage, and Laura will be near the goats.

Two sentences:

The Bengal tigers were quiet the whole time that they were on the stage.

The lions roared loudly.

Joining sentences by adding a conjunction:

The Bengal tigers were quiet the whole time that they were on the stage, but the lions roared loudly.

Let's Try It!
Set #6

Connect each group of two sentences (1 through 12) by using the conjunction *and*, *but*, or *so*.

1. Billy wanted to see the different areas in Grammar World.

   Laura wanted to stay in the water safari area.

   The combined sentence:

   _____

2. Scooter explored all areas of the animal kingdom.

   Riley spent the entire afternoon with Reptile Rob and his buddies.

   The combined sentence:

   _____

3. Rita rode the train in the early morning.
Daniel rode the train late in the evening.

The combined sentence:

_____

4. The students didn't want to leave the park at dusk.
The students stayed until midnight.

The combined sentence:

_____

5. The train slid into the noisy depot.
The train screeched as it came to a sudden stop.

The combined sentence:

_____

6. Five cars were added to the train at the end of the day.
A new engine was added the following night.

The combined sentence:

_____

7. Casey wants to go to the water park now.
Molly will go after the parade.

The combined sentence:

_____

8. Aaron visited Grammar World in the spring.
Aaron plans to return in the fall.

The combined sentence:

_____

9. Joe ran to the concession stand.
Lauren remained seated.

The combined sentence:

_____

10. Lions were loaded aboard the train.
Tigers were loaded aboard the train.
The bears were left behind.

The combined sentence:

_____

11. We were ready to see the rest of Grammar World.
Sabrina wanted to play with the animals a little longer.

The combined sentence:

_____

12. The students were going to trek into the forest.
They wore comfortable footwear.

The combined sentence:

_____

Answers are on page 141.

SENTENCE FRAGMENTS AND RUN-ON SENTENCES

SENTENCE FRAGMENTS

A sentence fragment does not express a complete thought. It is missing a subject or a verb.

A sentence fragment is like someone who has walked out the door without a shirt (the subject) or without pants (verb). Yikes! In either case, it's not a good look!

Sentence fragment: *watched an interesting movie about wildlife*

The subject is missing. Who or what is doing something? We don't know.

Complete sentence: *Kelsey watched an interesting movie about wildlife.*

A subject has been added. *Kelsey* is the subject.

Sentence fragment: *with all your favorite animal buddies*

Complete sentence: *Grammar World is brimming with all your favorite animal buddies.*

A subject and a predicate have been added. *Grammar World* is the subject, and *is brimming* is the predicate.

Sentence fragment: *back flips, tucks, and leaps*

Complete sentence: *Devin can do back flips, tucks, and leaps.*

A subject and a predicate have been added. *Devin* is the subject, and *can do* is the complete predicate.

Trick to Remember

Every sentence has two parts: a subject (the noun that the sentence is about) and a predicate (a verb that the subject is or did or is doing).

Let's Try It!
Set #7

Complete the following activity by doing what is asked.

Turn sentence fragments 1 through 6 into complete sentences by adding a subject and/or a predicate to each one.

1. Fragment: came face-to-face with an elephant

Sentence: _____

2. Fragment: grinned when she saw the parade of tropical fish

Sentence: _____

3. Fragment: When I met Shakespeare, he

Sentence: _____

4. Fragment: After the torrential downpour, the students were

Sentence: _____

5. Fragment: whistled while he peeled the bubble gum off his shoe

Sentence: _____

6. Fragment: made the audience giggle

Sentence: _____

Items 7 through 13 are a mix of both fragments and sentences. Correct any fragments by adding a subject and/or a predicate to each one. Write "no correction" if the numbered item is already a sentence. Remember to add an end punctuation mark.

7. Seventy-five barrels of chicken feed _____.

8. Flash photography is _____.

9. The underwater hippo viewing area was amazing _____.

10. When you trek into the forest _____.

11. _____ eye contact with a tiger.

12. _____ hundreds of wild, exotic, and rare animals.

13. _____ didn't feel so hot when they got off the safari bus.

Answers are on page 142.

RUN-ON SENTENCES

A run-on sentence contains two or more sentences that could stand alone. To correct a run-on sentence, add the proper punctuation or a connecting word like *and*, *but*, or *because*.

Run-on sentence:

We loved the Butterfly House and Kingdom it was as colorful as a rainbow.

Correct sentences:

We loved the Butterfly House and Kingdom. It was as colorful as a rainbow.

Run-on sentence:

Wear your wristband the whole time that you're at Grammar World it's your proof that you've paid for your ticket.

Correct sentences:

Wear your wristband the whole time that you're at Grammar World. It's your proof that you've paid for your ticket.

Wear your wristband the whole time that you're at Grammar World because it's your proof that you've paid for your ticket.

CAREFUL!

Not every run-on sentence is long. In fact, a run-on sentence can be short.

This is a run-on sentence: *I love dragons they are mythical creatures.*

This is <u>not</u> a run-on sentence: *If I could, I would spend every weekend at Grammar World and hang out in the dragon den.*

Let's Try It!
Set #8

Correct sentences 1 through 7 by adding the proper punctuation or a connecting word like *so*, *and*, or *but*.

1. Lauren wore a neon-green, stuffed snake around her neck she could be seen from a mile away.

2. On the way home we had a flat tire Haley fixed it.

3. After a fun-filled day at Grammar World, the children were tired they fell asleep quickly.

4. Shakespeare watched all the children arrive every morning he liked to wave to them as they entered Grammar World.

5. A loud noise exploded the fireworks were about to begin.

6. The train's whistle sounded like a bell the train's whistle sounded like a gong the train's whistle sounded like a scream.

7. Clay knew where all the rest stops were Cindy knew where all the rest stops were.

Answers are on page 143.

Let's Try It— Supersized!
Set #9

Are you ready for a big-time challenge? Shakespeare thinks so!

The following exercise contains fragments, run-on sentences, and sentences. If the boldface group of words is a fragment, add words that will make it a sentence. If it is a run-on sentence, add connecting words or punctuation. If it is already a complete sentence, draw a picture of Shakespeare smiling.

1. **likes to visit the bear and monkey exhibits**

_____

2. On Saturday, Mike and I went to the Wildlife Theatre we saw elephant shows.

_____

3. Jeff bought his tickets weeks before the show.

_____

4. knows how to soar like a bald eagle

_____

Answers are on page 144.

Wrapping It Up

In this chapter, you rode the theme park train around the park and got off at the sensational Sentence Station. You learned that a sentence is a group of words that expresses a complete thought. Every complete sentence begins with a capital letter and ends with a punctuation mark. Writers like you use declarative sentences more often than any other kind.

You also learned that a complete sentence has two parts: a subject and a predicate. The subject tells who or what the sentence is about. The predicate tells what the subject is or does. The verb is found in the predicate.

A sentence fragment does not express a complete thought. It is missing a subject or a verb.

Most writers don't write perfect sentences the first time around. The painless news is that you can reread and rework your fragments or sentences in different ways.

Let's Hit the Target!
Set #1

Here's a short story for you to read. After you have read the story, answer the questions in the boxes to see how well you understand sentences.

Once upon a time in Grammar World, there lived a chicken. This was no ordinary chicken, oh no! This chicken had a most unusual name—Shakespeare. Shakespeare watched over Grammar World. He especially loved seeing the children having fun.

> (1) Is this sentence a
> ❏ statement?
> ❏ question?
> ❏ command?
> ❏ exclamation?

(1) <u>One sunny day, Shakespeare decided to ride the train.</u> This doesn't sound like such a big deal until you think about how the other riders felt about having a chicken on board. One child squealed, (2) <u>"That chicken sure is funny!"</u>

> (2) Is this sentence a
> ❏ statement?
> ❏ question?
> ❏ command?
> ❏ exclamation?

Another child worried that Shakespeare might get hurt on the train ride. (3) "Be careful!" he said. "I don't want anything to happen to you."

Shakespeare was thrilled that the children were all using good grammar.

(4) "This is really a terrific group of kids!" Shakespeare crowed. (5) Soon the ride began.

Off they went on the Grammar World train ride. The children were having a wonderful time. They were able to see all the events happening in Grammar World. They saw the dolphin show, the rides, and the water park in the distance. (6) Everyone sang songs as the train traveled over hills and through tunnels. Suddenly the train (7) came to a screeching stop. What could be the problem? Shakespeare jumped off the train and went to investigate.

One of the children yelled to him, (8) "Hurry, Shakespeare, so the train can get going again we can see other stuff and ride the rides and go to the water park and the dolphin show."

"Hold your horses!" yelled Shakespeare. "You are using improper grammar! Let's try that again."

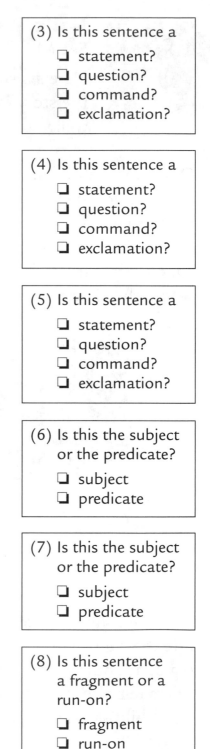

(3) Is this sentence a
- ❏ statement?
- ❏ question?
- ❏ command?
- ❏ exclamation?

(4) Is this sentence a
- ❏ statement?
- ❏ question?
- ❏ command?
- ❏ exclamation?

(5) Is this sentence a
- ❏ statement?
- ❏ question?
- ❏ command?
- ❏ exclamation?

(6) Is this the subject or the predicate?
- ❏ subject
- ❏ predicate

(7) Is this the subject or the predicate?
- ❏ subject
- ❏ predicate

(8) Is this sentence a fragment or a run-on?
- ❏ fragment
- ❏ run-on

"Hurry, Shakespeare, so that the train can get going again. We want to see other stuff. We want to ride the rides, go to the water park, and go to the dolphin show."

"That's much better!" exclaimed Shakespeare.

(9) "To the end?" asked a girl in the front train car.

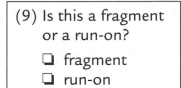

(9) Is this a fragment or a run-on?
❑ fragment
❑ run-on

Shakespeare asked her, "Do you mean, (10) "Can we ride the train to the end and see the animals?"

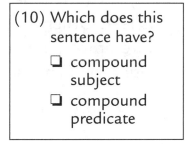

(10) Which does this sentence have?
❑ compound subject
❑ compound predicate

"Yes, that's what I meant."

"Absolutely," Shakespeare remarked. "Let's go. The train is fixed, and we are ready to roll."

(11) The children and Shakespeare hopped on board the train.

(11) Which does this sentence have?
❑ compound subject
❑ compound predicate

Answers are on page 144.

Fun Facts—Animals

Most kids enjoy learning about animals. Scientists who study animals are called zoologists. Would you like to be a zoologist one day?

Animals have adaptations that help them survive (live) in their environments. Here are some interesting facts about animals and their adaptations.

- Sea lions use their long, strong flippers to walk on land.

- A parrotfish uses mucus, which is like spit, to make a see-through sleeping bag around its body. The sleeping bag helps prevent other creatures from attacking it.

- A giraffe, the tallest mammal on the earth, often sleeps standing on its feet. Otherwise, it would take the animal too long to get up if, for example, a predator approaches. Would you like to sleep on your feet? (The author of this book wouldn't.)

- A river otter sends out a disgusting smell when threatened.

Fun Fact Follow-up

What is your favorite animal? Is it a monkey, ferret, seahorse, octopus, chicken, iguana, dragonfly, or some other creature? (Of course, Shakespeare hopes it's a chicken.)

Read some nonfiction books about an animal of your choice. You can also search the Web for information. Write down details about your animal such as what it eats and where it lives, along with the ways that it has adapted to the environment.

Once you have a good understanding of your topic, create an informational poster complete with illustrations about your animal. Remember to use the great skills you've been learning at Grammar World to make your writing wake up the jungle, rainforest, tundra, or habitat of your choice.

Chapter II

Nouns, Pronouns, and Adjectives—The Rides

Let's Go on the Rides!

Ride Restrictions:
Riders must strap themselves in and hold on.
They must want to improve their grammar.

Oh what fun it is to ride a ride at Grammar World!
Hmmm . . . did you notice anything different about that first sentence?
The word *ride* is used twice, first as a verb and then as a noun: "Oh
what fun it is to <u>ride</u> (verb) a <u>ride</u> (noun) at Grammar World!" Words
can be different parts of speech depending on how they are used in
sentences.

This chapter begins with a discussion about nouns. As you'll see,
Grammar World is full of nouns of all shapes and sizes. Sometimes
they are fast like the first <u>car</u> on the runaway <u>train</u>. Other times, they
are gentle like a slow, lazy <u>horse</u> on the <u>merry-go-round</u>.

COMMON AND PROPER NOUNS

COMMON NOUNS

A common noun names any person, place, thing, idea, or animal.

The <u>student</u> screamed when riding the roller <u>coaster</u> in the theme <u>park</u>.
    (person)   (thing)   (place)

Megan showed <u>kindness</u> to the lost <u>kitten</u>
          (idea)   (animal)

who was frightened by the booms of the bumper <u>cars</u>.
                                       (thing)

Cute little words like *a, an*, and *the* signal that a noun is ahead.

I want to ride the <u>cyclone</u>.

Please give me a <u>ticket</u>.

The noun does not always come right after the cute little word *a*, *and*, or *the*. Check out the following sentences!

I want to ride the biggest and fastest <u>cyclone</u> ever.

Please give me an admissions <u>bracelet</u>.

Not all nouns have cute little words to point them out. Some are proper nouns that, for example, name people like Shakespeare. You wouldn't say, "the Shakespeare." You would say "the fun-loving chicken."

Proper Nouns

A proper noun names a specific person, place, thing, idea, or animal. It always begins with a capital letter.

<u>*Tom*</u> *skateboarded in* <u>*Grammar World*</u>.
(specific person)   (specific place)

<u>*Benny the Bear*</u> *danced at the* <u>*Tilt-a-Whirl*</u>.
(specific animal)   (specific thing)

Trick to Remember

A common noun is capitalized only if it comes at the beginning of a sentence or if it is part of a title. A proper noun—such as a day of the week, a holiday, or a person's name—is always capitalized.

SINGULAR AND PLURAL NOUNS

The more the merrier. Here are some tips for changing a singular noun to a plural one.

Just add *s*

balloon	*balloons*
ride	*rides*
corn dog	*corn dogs*
horse	*horses*
ticket	*tickets*
scream	*screams*
volunteer	*volunteers*

Add *es* if the noun ends in *z*, *s*, *x*, *ch*, or *sh*.

a buzz	*many buzzes*
a mess	*several messes*
a box	*a stack of boxes*
a church	*two churches*
the beach	*the beaches*
a bush	*five bushes*
a dish	*three dishes*

If the noun ends in a consonant and *y*, change the *y* to *i* and add *es*.

country	*countries*
party	*parties*
kitty	*kitties*
baby	*babies*
city	*cities*
family	*families*
buddy	*buddies*
pony	*ponies*
cherry	*cherries*
fly	*flies*

If the noun ends in a vowel and *y*, just add *s*.

toy	*toys*
valley	*valleys*
monkey	*monkeys*
turkey	*turkeys*

Some nouns never change whether you are talking about one or a million and one.

a deer	*a gazillion deer*
a sheep	*a bijillion sheep*
a moose	*a gob of moose*
a fish	*a school of fish*

Some nouns have a special plural form.

a woman   *ten women*

a foot   *ten feet*

a mouse   *three blind mice*

one child   *six children*

a tooth   *a mouthful of teeth*

POSSESSIVE NOUNS

Mine! Mine! Mine! A possessive noun shows who or what owns something.

To make a singular noun possessive, just add an apostrophe and the letter *s*.

student   *the student's baseball cap*

child   *the child's ticket*

Jasmine   *Jasmine's popcorn*

ride operator   *the ride operator's gloves*

teacher   *the teacher's classroom list*

To make a plural noun possessive, check the last letter of the plural noun. If it is an *s*, just add an apostrophe.

leaders   *their leaders' line*

classmates   *the classmates' books*

riders   *those riders' tickets*

Bess   Bess' dress

students   the students' lunches

To make a plural noun possessive, check the last letter of the word. If it is not *s*, add *'s*.

mice   his mice's cheese

children   their children's seatbelts

men   the men's boots

sheep   the sheep's wool

Let's Try It!
Set #10

Complete 1 through 15 by doing what is asked.

Write the possessive form of each singular noun.

1. the water bottle of the student   the _____ water bottle

2. the rattle of the baby   the _____ rattle

3. the bone of the dog   the _____ bone

4. the script of the actor   the _____ script

5. the trunk of the elephant   the _____ trunk

6. the slime of the snail   the _____ slime

7. the fang of the snake   the _____ fang

Write the possessive form of each plural noun.

8. the horns of the deer   the _____ horns

9. the laughter of the women   the _____ laughter

10. the footballs of the teams   the _____ footballs

11. the whistles of the birds   the _____ whistles

12. the skis of the swimmers   the _____ skis

13. the antlers of the moose   the _____ antlers

14. the favorite rides of the children   the _____ favorite rides

15. the tickets of the riders   the _____ tickets

Answers are on page 144.

PRONOUNS

If it weren't for pronouns, writers often would have to use the same nouns over and over again. Take a look at the next paragraph.

Breaking news! This just in from the barnyard! Shakespeare has been named the honorary mayor of Grammar World. Shakespeare beat out the competition for many reasons. Shakespeare is one cool, calm, and collected chicken. Shakespeare doesn't allow anyone to ruffle Shakespeare's feathers. Shakespeare is also an awesome adventure guide. It's no wonder, then, that Shakespeare has earned the title of Honorary Mayor of Grammar World. Shall we refer to Shakespeare as Honorary Mayor Shakespeare?

Luckily for readers and writers, a pronoun takes the place of a noun. So, the pronouns *he*, *him*, and *his* can take the place of, or substitute for, *Shakespeare*. Take a peek at the new paragraph and you'll see the power of pronouns.

Breaking news! This just in from the barnyard! Shakespeare has been named the honorary mayor of Grammar World. <u>He</u> beat out the competition for many reasons. Shakespeare is one cool, calm, and collected chicken. <u>He</u> doesn't allow anyone to ruffle <u>his</u> feathers. Shakespeare is also an awesome adventure guide. It's no wonder, then, that <u>he</u> has earned the title of Honorary Mayor of Grammar World. Shall we refer to <u>him</u> as Honorary Mayor Shakespeare?

The addition of pronouns in the new paragraph helps it to flow more smoothly.

SUBJECT AND OBJECT PRONOUNS

SUBJECT PRONOUNS

A subject pronoun often comes at the beginning of the sentence. It tells whom or what the sentence is about.

<u>She</u> is going on the Great Gravity thrill ride.

<u>They</u> want to go on the Upside-Down Scrambler.

The chart below lists the subject pronouns.

Person	Singular	Plural
First person	*I*	*we*
Second person	*you*	*you*
Third person	*he, she, it*	*they*

Let's Try It!
Set #11

Complete 1 through 15 by doing what is asked.

Underline the subject pronoun in sentences 1–8.

1. I rode the Shakespeare Skyscraper after the sun went down.

2. You can go to Grammar World with us next week.

3. We will take five buses on the field trip.

4. They want to play football at Grammar World.

5. It is the first day of spring.

6. She is one of the funniest clowns.

7. He will visit Grammar World during his spring break next year.

8. They saw Shakespeare eating a foot-long hot dog on the Ferris wheel.

For 9 through 15, add a subject pronoun that makes sense.

9. Mary Jane and Keith want to ride the Shakespeare Shaker. _____ will have to buy tickets for the ride.

10. Tim's entire football team went to Grammar World. _____ had a terrific time.

11. Haley and the cast rode the alligator ride for three hours. _____ rode the alligator ride until after dark.

12. Scott is on the ride. _____ will return soon.

13. Shea and Adrianna were fascinated with the upside-down ride. _____ couldn't believe their eyes!

14. Shakespeare helped the girls find the best seats on the merry-go-round. _____ loved seeing the smiles on their faces.

15. The stray cat found its way into Grammar World and searched for something to eat. _____ was happy when it found bits of hot dog and potato chips around the trash barrel.

Answers are on page 145.

OBJECT PRONOUNS

An object pronoun often comes at the end of the sentence. It often follows an action verb or preposition.

*Shakespeare rescued **me**.*

*Shakespeare bought double chocolate milk shakes for **them**. De-lish!*

The chart below lists the object pronouns.

Person	Singular	Plural
First person	*me*	*us*
Second person	*you*	*you*
Third person	*him, her, it*	*them*

Here's an Idea

To figure out if a pronoun is a subject or an object pronoun, try putting a preposition (like the word *to*) in front of the pronoun. If the preposition and pronoun sound right together, the pronoun is an object pronoun.

*I will give the ball to **she**.*

The pronoun *she* does not sound right here. *She* is a subject pronoun.

*I will give the ball to **her**.*

Bingo! The pronoun her sounds fine here, so it is an object pronoun.

Let's Try It!
Set #12

<u>Underline</u> the object pronoun in each of the following sentences (1 through 6).

1. Isabella ran away from us.

2. The monkey will throw the peanut to him.

3. All the performers sang to us.

4. Shakespeare found the right answer on the grammar test and drew an orange circle around it.

5. Please give the big, green ball to me so that we can play water polo.

6. Shea told Adrianna to give the ball to her.

Fill in the correct object pronoun for 7 through 12.

7. The clown ran to Tracy and _____ (me, you).

8. Kelsey gave the cotton candy to _____ (she, her).

9. The monkey ran to Shakespeare and _____ (him, he).

10. Molly wanted the Frisbee, so Casey threw it to _____ (she, her).

11. When the clowns walked by, we laughed at _____ (they, them).

12. Keith saw Lauren and gave his ticket to ___ (she, her).

Answers are on page 145.

POSSESSIVE PRONOUNS

The next story will not only entertain you but will also teach you about possessive pronouns.

One sunny day in Grammar World, Shakespeare was busy painting the rides. He wanted to make them look fresh and new. Two adorable girls, Adrianna and Shea, noticed what he was doing and stopped to chat.

"What are you doing, Shakespeare? Can we help?" asked the girls. "We are good painters." (The girls had helped **_their_** parents paint <u>their</u> garages, so they were experienced.)

"That would be great," replied Shakespeare. "**_My_** idea is to paint all the rides so that they look bright and appealing."

"Are all these rides **_yours_**?" Adrianna and Shea asked.

"I feel like the rides and everything here at Grammar World are **_mine_** because I care about them so much," Shakespeare said.

Just then, the girls noticed that Shakespeare had spilled paint on **_his_** beautiful white feathers. Adrianna took a tissue out of *her* backpack and wiped the paint off **his** feathers.

"Thanks, girls. I really appreciate *your* help," Shakespeare said with a smile.

"You're welcome," responded the girls. "**Our** parents would be proud of us for helping out."

After reading the story, can you describe in your own words what a possessive pronoun is?

A possessive pronoun takes the place of a possessive noun. The chart below lists the possessive pronouns.

Person	Singular	Plural
First person	*my, mine*	*our, ours*
Second person	*your, yours*	*your, yours*
Third person	*his, her, hers, its*	*their, theirs*

Some possessive pronouns can be used before nouns.

Find Anne's ticket.

Find her ticket.

Luke and Laura's favorite ride at Grammar World is the Swirl and Twirl.

Their favorite ride at Grammar World is the Swirl and Twirl.

Some possessive pronouns stand alone.

The ticket is Lindsey's.

The ticket is hers.

Let's Try It!

Set #13

<u>Underline</u> the possessive pronoun in each sentence.

1. Kathy stood in line for her favorite ride.

2. Caroline liked her movie-star sunglasses, which she bought at Grammar World.

3. At dark, Peter saw his best friend.

4. Shakespeare wiped the paint from his white feathers.

5. Don't chew with your mouth open!

6. We did not know where our class was going.

Answers are on page 146.

⌐ Careful!

Sometimes contractions and possessive pronouns look alike. In the sentence "*You're* going to help *your* sister," the contraction *you're* stands for *you are*. It is different from the possessive pronoun *your*.

ADJECTIVES

Would it surprise you if I told you that Shakespeare likes to dress up as his favorite adjective? Well, it's true. Yesterday, Shakespeare showed up at the main gates of Grammar World dressed up as a <u>large</u>, <u>purple</u> Martian. Today, he came dressed as a <u>grouchy</u>, <u>black</u> cat. No one except Shakespeare knows what adjective he'll be tomorrow. It depends on his mood.

Adjectives are describing words. They describe nouns, as in the phrase <u>sharp</u>, <u>loud</u>, <u>spooky</u> sounds. <u>Awesome</u> authors like you use describing words to liven up their writing pieces and to help readers create pictures in their minds.

Adjectives add spice to words and sentences. Without them, language would be bland and boring. Imagine popcorn without salt. Imagine nachos without salsa. Just like food without seasoning,

writing would lack flavor without adjectives. Take, for example, the bland sentence "Shea rode the ride." Let's try flavoring it with a few adjectives as follows: "Shea rode the <u>wild</u> and <u>bumpy log</u> ride" or even "<u>Brave</u> Shea rode the <u>monstrous log</u> ride."

Here is an entire treasure chest of adjectives you can use. There is also room in the treasure chest for you to add your favorite describing words.

ancient (old)	juicy	dry	favorite
frozen	warm	humid	dusty
dry	sunny	wet	rainy
all the color words			
all the size words (large, small, huge, tiny, gigantic)			
spooky	playful	funny	grumpy
angry	cheerful	fancy	quiet
_____	_____	_____	_____

Little words like *a*, *an*, and *the* are also adjectives. You can remember that fact, right? Great, because then we can focus on the main or really juicy describing words. See for yourself. Check out the boldface adjectives in the following sentences.

*The **haunted** house looked **ancient**. (Remember, <u>the</u> is also an adjective.)*

*Let's go on the ride with the **biggest** and **scariest** drop.*

*The **Floridian** peaches were **juicy**.*

Let's Try It!
Set #14

Put a box around the adjectives in the following sentences.

1. Little Riley cried when the tiny, yellow toy boats floated past him.

2. The beautiful full moon shone on Grammar World at midnight.

3. Last Saturday, Molly decided to visit the haunted castle.

4. Five students screamed as the fantastic blue bus flew by.

5. Shakespeare painted beautiful, bright numbers on all the new bumper cars.

6. When she was in the scary fun house, Shea came face to face with a large make-believe bat.

Draw a <u>line</u> under each adjective and draw a <u>circle</u> around the noun it describes.

7. One happy girl will ride the fast roller coaster.

8. Nervous students laughed during the dark part of the scary ride.

9. Blue dolphins swam around the sloppy log ride.

10. A funny animal movie was shown at Grammar World.

11. The <u>hilarious</u> play was about goofy animals of all shapes and sizes.

12. We saw purple popping penguins, yellow yawning yaks, and silvery slimy snakes.

Answers are on page 146.

ARTICLES

Articles are the little words that signal nouns. They are the special words *a*, *an*, and *the*. Articles are actually a special type of adjective. They are small but mighty.

The article **a** signals that a noun beginning with a consonant sound is coming.

A favorite ride at Grammar World is Bumper Cars.

The article **an** signals that a noun beginning with a vowel sound is coming.

An animal ride is fun for younger children.

The article **the** can be used before any noun.

The Beast is the scariest ride of all.

ADJECTIVES AFTER LINKING VERBS

When an adjective follows the noun it describes, the noun and adjective are connected by a linking verb.

The <u>rides</u> are <u>frightening</u>.
(noun)   (adjective)

The <u>kids</u> were <u>excited</u>.
(noun)   (adjective)

Let's Try It!
Set #15

Practice makes perfect. Complete 1 through 10 by doing what is asked.

For sentences 1 through 4, draw a line under the <u>adjective</u> and two lines under the <u>noun</u> it describes.

1. Grammar World was busy with happy visitors.

2. The purple grape slurpie was refreshing to the hot, exhausted child.

3. The haunted castle was filled with screaming people.

4. The fifth-grade students were thrilled to be riding such incredible rides.

In sentences 5 through 10, the nouns are underlined. Find the adjectives and underline them twice.

5. Sandy decided to visit the concession <u>stand</u> to buy a yummy funnel <u>cake</u>.

6. The <u>moon</u> was red and glowing at night.

7. The summer <u>weather</u> was unpredictable.

8. His large, black <u>hat</u> is missing.

9. Her cherry <u>cola</u> was frosty and refreshing.

10. <u>Todd</u> saw a gray <u>mouse</u> running through the dark fun <u>house</u>.

Answers are on page 147.

ADJECTIVES THAT COMPARE

Adjectives are also helpful when you are comparing things. For example, if you are reading the story "Goldilocks and the Three Bears," you might say that Baby Bear is big, Mama Bear is bigger, and Papa Bear is the biggest. When you are comparing **two** things to each other, you use the two letters *er*.

Mama Bear is bigger than Baby Bear.

The rides at Grammar World are wilder than those at other theme parks.

When you are comparing **three or more** things to each other, use the three letters *est.*

Papa Bear is the biggest of all.

The rides at Grammar World are the wildest in the universe.

Some adjectives need a little *more* help to make a comparison.

Put *more* and *most* before adjectives to show comparisons.

Use *more* to compare two or more things.

Use *most* to compare three or more things.

spectacular	*more spectacular*	*most spectacular*
beautiful	*more beautiful*	*most beautiful*
brilliant	*more brilliant*	*most brilliant*

Let's Try It!
Set #16

Complete sentences 1 through 8 by adding the word more or most.

1. The Grammar Gremlin is _____ fun to ride than the swings.

2. Adrianna was the _____ tired of all the children.

3. Shakespeare is _____ friendly than his barnyard buddies.

4. Lindsay ate _____ bubble gum ice cream than Tim.

5. Todd ate the _____ ice cream of all.

6. Grammar World is _____ entertaining than other theme parks.

7. Devin is the _____ impressive cheerleader.

8. Our city's parks are the _____ beautiful in the state.

Answers are on page 147.

CONTRACTIONS

A contraction is a shortened form of one or two words that uses an apostrophe to replace one or more letters. The apostrophe is placed at the spot where the letter(s) has been removed. Often a contraction is formed by joining a pronoun with a verb.

He is standing in line.   *He's standing in line.*

Sometimes a contraction is formed by joining a verb with *not*.

He is not standing on line.   *He isn't standing on line.*

Meaning	Contraction	Meaning	Contraction
I am	I'm	they are	they're
I will	I'll	they will	they'll
I would/had	I'd	they have	they've
I have	I've	there is	there's
you are	you're	are not	aren't
you will	you'll	was not	wasn't
you have	you've	were not	weren't
he is/has	he's	will not	won't
he will	he'll	would not	wouldn't
he would/had	he'd	cannot	can't
she is/has	she's	could not	couldn't
she will	she'll	did not	didn't
she would/had	she'd	does not	doesn't
we are	we're	do not	don't
we will	we'll	had not	hadn't
we would/had	we'd	has not	hasn't
we have	we've	is not	isn't
it is/has	it's	should not	shouldn't

Let's Try It!

Set #17

Change the underlined words in each sentence to a contraction.

1. Scott said that <u>he would</u> go to Grammar Canyon with me.

2. <u>I am</u> not afraid of heights, so let's go on the swing ride.

3. <u>She is</u> feeling dizzy.

4. <u>He will</u> buy an all-season pass to Grammar World.

5. <u>Do not</u> be surprised if Shakespeare shows up.

Answers are on page 148.

Wrapping It Up

Colorful nouns, pronouns, and adjectives can spice up a piece of lifeless writing. But this does not mean that you should toss any old noun, pronoun, or adjective onto the written page or computer screen. Great writers like you choose their parts of speech carefully. They know that too many adjectives, for example, can make their pieces sound strange or unnatural, as in the phrase <u>beautiful, sweet, smart, kind, talented, friendly</u> students.

Pronouns are helpful because they cut down on the number of times that writers have to use the same noun over again. So, for example, the pronoun *he* can substitute for *Shakespeare*. The pronoun *it* can take the place of *Grammar World*.

Let's Hit the Target!
Set #2

Let's put your knowledge to use. Read the following story. Then answer the questions in the boxes to see how well you understand nouns, pronouns, and adjectives.

It was a typical day in Grammar World. (1) <u>Shakespeare</u> was busy watching over the visitors and making sure everyone was having an enjoyable time.

Suddenly, a loud (2) <u>crash</u> was heard at the rides. What was happening?

The Ferris wheel had gotten stuck. It had come to a dead stop with three (3) <u>children</u> at the very top. (4) <u>They</u> were screaming at the top of their lungs, "Help!"

Shakespeare arrived at the scene in the nick of time. (5) "<u>I</u> will save you!" he yelled to the frightened children. He knew he had to get (6) <u>them</u> help quickly.

He ran back to the barn where the Grammar World (7) <u>equipment</u> was kept. There he found a special truck with a ladder long enough to reach the children. As quick as a wink, Shakespeare jumped in the truck and

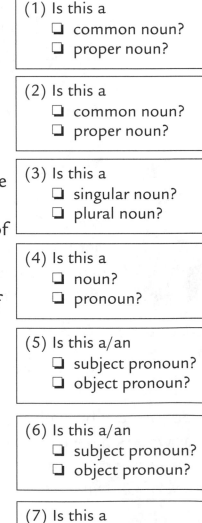

(1) Is this a
❏ common noun?
❏ proper noun?

(2) Is this a
❏ common noun?
❏ proper noun?

(3) Is this a
❏ singular noun?
❏ plural noun?

(4) Is this a
❏ noun?
❏ pronoun?

(5) Is this a/an
❏ subject pronoun?
❏ object pronoun?

(6) Is this a/an
❏ subject pronoun?
❏ object pronoun?

(7) Is this a
❏ common noun?
❏ proper noun?

drove it to the Ferris wheel. He jumped out of the truck and pulled out the ladder.

Shakespeare flew up the ladder, scooped up the crying children, and carefully brought them down. When they reached the ground, everyone was happy. Then one of the girls began sobbing. (8) <u>She</u> had left her favorite doll on the (9) <u>Ferris wheel</u> seat.

Shakespeare did not hesitate for (10) <u>a</u> moment. He scrambled back up the ladder, snatched the doll, and returned to the ground. He was a hero. The girl told Shakespeare that he had turned this into the (11) <u>happiest</u> day of her life.

"I (12) <u>can't</u> tell you how happy you have made me today!" the girl exclaimed.

Shakespeare just smiled. It was another great day in Grammar World!

Answers are on page 148.

(8) Is this a
❏ subject pronoun?
❏ object pronoun?

(9) Is this a
❏ common noun?
❏ proper noun?

(10) Is this an
❏ article?
❏ noun?

(11) Is this a
❏ adjective?
❏ article?

(12) Is this a
❏ contraction?
❏ conjunction?

NEW RIDES AT GRAMMAR WORLD

Grammar World has two new rides: the Wheel of Nouns and the Adjective Avalanche. Read about them in the following story. When you're finished reading, use a highlighter and make all the nouns blue, the pronouns pink, and the adjectives green.

Adrianna and Shea spent hours riding all the rides at Grammar World. Their first stop was the Wheel of Nouns, where riders get to choose from many different people, places, and things to ride. There were statues of famous people, like George Washington, maps of interesting places to climb, like Mt. Everest, and unique things to crawl inside, like jellyfish and trolley cars.

After that, the girls headed for the Adjective Avalanche, where riders choose different hills and valleys to visit and design them any way they wish. The hills and valleys could be black, white, orange, or any other color of the rainbow. They could be tall, short, skinny, or wide. They could be shiny, dull, rough, or smooth. The choices were all Adrianna's and Shea's to make. How exciting!

After going on the rides, the girls were happy, tired, and also starving. It seemed like forever since they had gobbled down a doughnut and some chocolate milk for breakfast. They decided to search for a lunch that was out of the ordinary—something unusual. They passed hot dog stands, pizza places, and fancy restaurants. Nothing seemed right. Then they saw it—the Noun Nook. At first they thought it sounded weird, until they looked at the menu.

Just as you can't judge a book by its cover, you can't judge a restaurant by its name. The Noun Nook was an amazing place filled with foods from all over the world. There were crispy noodles from Japan, hearty soups from Russia, scones from Great Britain, flan puddings from Mexico, bubbling pastas from Italy, special chocolate cookies from Switzerland, piping hot apple pie from the United States, and much, much more. The girls were delighted and soon stuffed themselves with delicious foods.

Armed with full tummies and bursting with excitement, the girls paused a moment to plan their next move. The day had gotten very hot. The water park seemed like the best choice, and so off they went.

As Adrianna glanced back to take one last look at all the mild and wild rides, she spotted what she thought was a chicken. Where had she seen such a chicken before? Of course, it was the same chicken that had been in her dream just last night—the same dream Shea had also had. Could she have seen the chicken again here at Grammar World? Impossible!

Shea started to tell Adrianna what she had seen but was stopped unexpectedly when both girls crashed headlong into their best friends from school, Devin and Kelsey. What luck! They all could go to the water park together and have twice the fun!

As the foursome walked away, a strange creature watched them with great interest. It was a chicken!

Fun Facts—Roller Coasters

Imagine this. You're barreling down the track of a roller coaster at 80 miles per hour. Within seconds, your stomach drops to your knees and scary thoughts fill your head. You say to yourself, "Self. A seatbelt is the only thing that is keeping me from danger." But are your thoughts really true?

Luckily for you, and for roller coaster fans, you're in less danger than you think. Thanks to the science of physics, roller coasters are designed to give you the feeling of danger rather than the actual experience of it. Whew!

The roller coaster has no engine. After the first hill at the beginning of the ride, the coaster completes the whole ride on its own. Physics—which includes the study of friction, gravity, and energy—plays a big role in the workings of a roller coaster.

Fun Fact Follow-up
The history of roller coasters is as thrilling as the rides themselves. Read some nonfiction books about roller coasters. You can also seek out information on the Web. Write a summary of the origins (beginnings) of roller coasters. In your summary, be sure to include the different names given to roller coasters over time and descriptions of each ride.

Verbs and Adverbs—
The Water Park

Ride Restrictions:
All riders must wear sunscreen and a life jacket.
All riders must want to improve their grammar.

Brave the Waves.

Words can be different parts of speech depending on how they are used in sentences. Take a look at the next sentence.

Oh what fun it is to wave at Shakespeare braving a humongous wave!

Notice that the word *wave* is used twice, first as a verb and then as a noun: "Oh what fun it is to <u>wave</u> (verb) at Shakespeare braving a humongous <u>wave</u> (noun)!"

A sentence without a verb is like a water park without water. It is missing an important, needed part. Verbs tell what is happening in a sentence. Every complete sentence must have a verb. I <u>mean</u> it! I <u>am</u> not kidding!

One strong verb goes a long way in driving the energy and power of a sentence.

If you want to make a splash with your writing, choose your verbs carefully!

Not all verbs are the same. Dive into the next few pages and see the differences for yourself.

ACTION VERBS

Raced! Hiked! Leaped! Can you guess what these words are doing? They are expressing action. Words like these are called action verbs.

Action verbs are sure to **grab** the reader's attention. They put subjects into motion. Action verbs tell what somebody or something does, did, or will do.

Molly <u>jumped</u> into the swimming pool.

<u>Molly</u> = subject; <u>jumped</u> = action verb [**jumped** puts Molly into action.]

Riley <u>dove</u> into the deepest part of the pool.

Shakespeare <u>hit</u> the water with a belly smacker.

You can find a lot of action words in the sports pages of a newspaper.

Hannah <u>smashed</u> the softball.

Peter <u>dribbled</u> the basketball.

Haley <u>scored</u> a touchdown.

Sally <u>kicked</u> a field goal.

Alessandria <u>cheered</u> for hours.

Trick to Remember

Action verbs are mighty and powerful! Great writers like you use action verbs in their writing pieces whenever it makes sense to do so.

LINKING VERBS

Linking verbs are like bubble gum on the bottom of your shoe. They stick things together. Check out the following sentences and see for yourself.

*Tyler **is** excited about meeting his friends at Grammar World.*

*Shakespeare **will be** happy when all the children arrive.*

*Lauren and Scott **were** sunburned at the end of the day.*

*Keith **has been** sad about leaving the water park.*

Linking verbs connect the subject of a verb to other information about the subject. Some of the most common linking verbs are *am*, *is*, *are*, *was*, *were*, *seem*, and *become*.

Trick to Remember

Linking verbs tell what something or somebody is, was, or will be. They are also known as *being verbs*.

Action-packed verbs are stronger and more vivid than linking verbs. Whenever possible (and it is not always possible), try to use action verbs in your writing. So, *"Shakespeare <u>was</u> happy."* might become *"Shakespeare <u>squawked</u> with delight."*

HELPING VERBS

Some helping verbs help the main verb of a sentence. Others stand alone and act as the main verb.

Helping verbs like *should, must,* and *would* help the main verb.

Shakespeare <u>should</u> use his life jacket to go tubing.

(*should*— helping verb; *use*—main verb)

Helping verbs like *are* and *can* may also stand alone and be the main verb of a sentence.

You <u>are</u> wet.

are—main verb

You <u>are getting</u> wet.

are—helping verb; *getting*—main verb

Helping verbs give readers clues as to when the action of a sentence takes place.

Todd <u>has</u> made seven foul shots in a row.

The action took place in the **past**.

Devin <u>will</u> perform a back flip.

The action will take place in the **future**.

Trick to Remember

If you want to hunt for helping verbs, be on the lookout for *ing* verbs such as *riding* and *gliding* and *sliding*. They signal you that a helping verb is nearby. Do you understand what I <u>am</u> saying?

ADVERBS

Adverbs give additional information about verbs. They tell when, how, why, or where an action takes place. Adverbs that tell how often usually end in *ly*.

> <u>Yesterday</u>, I went to Grammar World.
>
> Molly <u>quickly</u> slid down the slide.
>
> Carley screamed <u>loudly</u> as she dove off the high dive.

Below is an entire treasure chest of adverbs you can use.

Adverbs that tell when:

last	first	never	then
now	tomorrow	next	early

Adverbs that tell how:

quickly	happily	sadly	suddenly
slowly	rapidly	badly	sluggishly

Adverbs that tell where:

far	around	here	inside
everywhere	there	up	

Let's Try It!

Set #18

Now it is time to show all you know about action verbs, linking verbs, helping verbs, and adverbs. Complete 1 through 20 by doing what is asked in each section. GO!

Choose an action verb for these sentences that makes sense. Many answers are possible.

1. Lauren _____ across the road to reach the other side.

2. Peter _____ the baseball out of the pool.

3. Tyler _____ the floor after we slipped on Jello.

4. Will Alex _____ to the water ride before he leaves?

5. On Saturday, Shakespeare _____ before dark.

Choose a linking verb for these sentences that makes sense. Many answers are possible.

6. Kelsey _____ an actor at Grammar World.

7. Kelly _____ the new water shooter.

8. The best day for the boat race _____ Saturday.

9. Cory _____ sure that he would be the first one on the bus to Grammar World.

10. They _____ athletic.

Choose a helping verb for these sentences that makes sense.

11. Kathy wished she _____ attend the dance at Grammar World.

12. Aaron _____ marry the water park princess.

13. Shawn _____ drive the bus to the field trip.

14. Will Portia _____ enough money to swim all day long?

15. Because she has a cold, Molly _____ not get to go to the evening swimming performance.

Choose an adverb for these sentences that makes sense. (There is a treasure chest of adverbs you can go to for ideas on page 69.)

16. Peter _____ ran down the hill to reach the pool.

17. Dillon knew _____ that he was going to have a great time.

18. _____, Lindsey was chilled to the bone.

19. Kelsey and Devin _____ decided that they would stay until the fireworks show ended.

20. Shakespeare _____ waved good-bye to all the children as they left Grammar World.

Complete the following sentences by using an action verb, linking verb, helping verb, or adverb.

21. _Action verb:_ The principal _____ Portia into her office.

22. _Linking verb:_ Tracy _____ at the water park.

23. _Helping verb:_ Lois _____ join the swim team.

24. _Adverb:_ _____, Tom watched the dolphin show with his friend.

Answers are on page 148.

STRONG VERBS VERSUS WEAK VERBS

It's time to **pump up** your writing with powerful verbs and transform weak sentences to strong, interesting ones.

Read the following sentence pairs. Notice how a strong verb makes a sentence more interesting.

I was happy at Grammar World.

I smiled and laughed out loud at Grammar World.

Shakespeare looked at the children.

Shakespeare guarded the childen.

Adrianna and Shea are at the water park.

Adrianna and Shea slide and splash at the water park.

Isabella was unhappy when it was time to leave.

Isabella screamed, pouted, and stomped her foot when it was time to leave.

As you can see, strong verbs help to make your writing fun to read. Whenever you can, and whenever it makes sense to do so, use vivid verbs in your writing pieces. If you do, your words will <u>splash</u> off the pages and your readers will <u>jump</u> for joy and <u>dive</u> in for more.

Do you know what time it is? It's time to read an entertaining story that is filled with colorful and vivid verbs. After you read the story, put a circle around five of your favorite verbs.

The Wonders of the Water

As Adrianna and Shea frantically raced toward the water park, they talked excitedly with their best friends, Devin and Kelsey, about the fun that they were going to have.

All year long at school, Adrianna and Shea had been dreaming of this great adventure and imagining that their playground was a water park. During recess, when they went down the slide on the playground, they had secretly pretended that they were racing down waterslides. Adrianna and Shea also pretended that the teeter-totter was a tube ride because it went up and down, and the monkey bars were like water trapezes.

It had been so much fun thinking about the trip to Grammar World. And now the fun was really here. To make a wonderful day even better, the girls had run into their best friends, Kelsey and Devin, who had agreed to go to the water park with them. Life was good. No, life was GREAT!

As they neared the water park, the foursome decided that they should put on sunscreen. After applying the lotion, the children decided to go down the spiral slide. Adrianna was the first one to climb the 236 steps to the top of the tower. Shea, Devin, and Kelsey followed closely behind. When they reached the top, they each took a deep breath before launching themselves down the dark tunnel to the pool below. Adrianna screamed at the top of her lungs, and Shea held her breath. Devin and Kelsey could also be heard making loud noises.

When the children reached the bottom of the tunnel, they collapsed into fits of laughter. Immediately they sprang to their feet, climbed the stairs, and took another turn on the spiral slide. This time, the boys went first. The children repeated this activity many times. Each trip brought even more laugher and fun.

Next, the foursome visited the Verb Vortex. Just think of a verb, and you could do it on this ride! The children climbed, slid, wiggled, bolted, swam, plunged, and even catapulted. Just think of an exciting adverb and that describes how the children moved about in the Verb Vortex. They went quickly, swiftly, fearlessly, joyously, smoothly, and noisily, because of all the screaming.

Finally, Adrianna suggested that they try the waterslide, so off they went. Kelsey had been to Grammar World many times before and knew the best way to achieve the fastest ride down the slide. He instructed the other three on how to position their mats, and off they went. They traveled so quickly down the slide, it was as if they were flying! Adrianna's long, blond hair stuck straight out from behind her head. As soon as they reached the base of the slide, they raced back up to the top for another turn.

Two hours passed. The children were exhausted and ready for a rest. Devin and Kelsey said good-bye to the girls. They had to find their parents and return home for a soccer game. Adrianna and Shea decided to visit the ice cream shop before going on to the dolphin show. They chatted about what kind of ice cream they would get. It would not be an easy decision, as the shop offered more than 100 flavors. Yum!

Adrianna and Shea stuffed themselves with ice cream. They had a difficult time deciding on what flavor to choose. After all, there were 100! At first, Adrianna had wanted double-double chocolate chip cherry cheesecake delight. Then she changed her mind and decided upon pineapple coconut kiwi pistachio island delight with juju worms and sprinkles. Shea ordered vanilla. Both girls had eaten their ice cream so quickly that they had "frozen headaches," so they decided to find a shady place and rest.

What an amazing day it had been! The best part was that there was still more fun to be had. As the girls rested on the bench, they quietly discussed their next stop: the Dolphin Show. Adrianna knew that this would be Shea's favorite part of the day. Shea had wanted to be a marine biologist since forever, and aquatic animals interested her greatly. The walls of her bedroom at home were completely covered with posters of all kinds of sea life.

Suddenly, Shea had the strangest feeling that someone was secretly watching them. She told Adrianna how she felt, and to Shea's surprise, Adrianna said she also felt the very same way.

After looking around and finding nothing out of the ordinary, the girls finally decided to head over to the dolphin show. Off they went to what they felt would be one of the highlights of their day. High overhead in a tree, a chicken silently watched the girls walk away.

VERB TENSES

It's about time that we discussed verb tenses because verb tenses are all about time.

The three main verb tenses are past, present, and future. They tell you when the actions of the verbs take place.

A verb is in the **present tense** when it tells something that is happening right now.

Now I run.

I am swimming right this very second.

Today I am going to visit Grammar World.

A verb is in the **past tense** when it tells something that happened in the past.

Yesterday I ran.

I was swimming last week.

On Monday, I visited Grammar World.

A verb is in the **future tense** when it tells something that will happen in the future.

Tomorrow I will run.

Next year my family and I will go swimming.

We will travel to Grammar World soon.

Let's Try It!

Set #19

Complete 1 through 19 by doing what is asked.

Figure out the tense of the verb for sentences 1 through 10. Then, depending on the verb tense, write the number *1* (present tense), *2* (past tense), or *3* (future tense) in the space provided.

1. ___ Kathy **decided** to swim down the water tunnel on her stomach.

2. ___ Lois **will jump** into the icy-cold pool of blue water.

3. ___ Shakespeare **is watching** all the action from the side of the pool.

4. ___ Riley **will return** to Grammar World as soon as his parents let him.

5. ___ Dillon **decided** to buy a new swim suit for the class trip.

6. ___ The entire football team **crowded** into the baby pool with Shakespeare.

7. ___ Shakespeare **is** on a surfboard.

8. ___ On Saturday, the pools **were drained** in order to clean them.

9. ___ Tom and Devin **were competing** against each other to see who could make the biggest splash.

10. ___ Tom **won**.

Use the verb *walk* to show each verb tense below. You may need to use a helping verb too.

11. **Future:** Scooter _____ to school tomorrow.

12. **Past:** Cory _____ to school yesterday.

13. **Present:** Tyler _____ to school today.

Use the verb *splash* to show each verb tense below. You may need to use a helping verb too.

14. **Future:** Karry _____ in the pool tomorrow.

15. **Past:** Joe _____ in the pool yesterday.

16. **Present:** Tracy _____ in the pool today.

Use the verb *slide* to show each verb tense below. You may need to use a helping verb too.

17. **Future:** Tracy _____ down the water tunnel tomorrow.

18. **Past:** Kelly _____ down the water tunnel yesterday.

19. **Present:** Shakespeare _____ down the water tunnel today.

Answers are on page 149.

SUBJECT-VERB AGREEMENT

Can't we all just get along! When a subject and verb do not agree, it's like two people having a loud argument. It's not pretty.

Check out the examples below. Shakespeare thinks you'll agree that when subjects and verbs agree, sentences sound so much better.

Incorrect: *Fourth-graders enjoys visiting water parks.*
  Correct: *Fourth-graders enjoy visiting water parks.*

Incorrect: *All the students rushes home after school.*
  Correct: *All the students rush home after school.*

Incorrect: *The new bubble gum snap.*
  Correct: *The new bubble gum snaps.*

Incorrect: *Casey launch a water balloon from the tower.*
  Correct: *Casey launched a water balloon from the tower.*

Incorrect: *After school is out, many of the students enjoys splashing in swimming pools.*
  Correct: *After school is out, many of the students enjoy splashing in swimming pools.*

Incorrect: *Shakespeare enjoy seeing all the children at Grammar World.*
  Correct: *Shakespeare enjoys seeing all the children at Grammar World.*

- Verbs must agree with their subjects.

- If the subject is single, you can add *s* to most present tense verbs. If the word ends in *ch, sc, x, z,* or *s,* add *es.*

- If the subject is *I* or *you*, do not add *s* or *es.*

Let's Try It!
Set #20

Choose the present tense verb form that matches the subject in each sentence.

1. Lauren and Scott (write, writes) about the water park in their journals.

2. Adrianna (watch, watches) the swimmers jump into the waterfall.

3. Molly always (wish, wishes) upon a star at the fireworks show.

4. Joe (wax, waxes) his surfboard every day.

5. Tyler (will buy, is buying) cool Hawaiian swimming trunks for the trip.

6. Peter (is taking, took) a good book to read because he has to stay out of the sun.

7. The entire class (swam, is swimming) at night under the strobe lights.

8. Cory (rode, rides) a wave.

9. Today, Scooter (races, raced) to be the first in line.

10. Now I see how much fun we (are having, had).

Answers are on page 150.

IRREGULAR VERBS

Weird! Wild! Unpredictable!

Irregular verbs do not add *ed* to form the past tense.

An irregular verb lives up to its name. It's just not predictable.

This chart lists some of the most common irregular verbs.

Present	Past	Past with Helping Verbs
begin	began	begun
do	did	done
come	came	come
eat	ate	eaten
fly	flew	flown
freeze	froze	frozen
lie	lay	lain
swim	swam	swum
drink	drank	drunk

Treasure Hunt

Hidden in the following story are several verbs. Can you find them? Underline any verbs you discover and record your number in the box below. Remember, there are three kinds of verbs: action, linking, and helping.

The water park was busy, busy, busy one hot and steamy August day. Everyone had the same idea of visiting Grammar World and cooling off at the refreshing water park. Children and adults alike were swooshing and splashing and having a grand old time.

Suddenly, a gigantic whirlpool formed and water began to spin and swirl like a tornado.

What could be causing this? Was it a faulty drain? Maybe it was a weird windstorm of some sort. Everyone tried to get out of the water, but the current was too strong.

How many verbs did you find? Write your number in the box below. Compare your answer with a friend's.

How many verbs did you find? Write your number in the box below. Compare your answer with a friend's.

Now for the really fun part: You get to finish the story. Gosh, I can't wait to see how you deal with this phenomenon. OK. What happened next? Oh yes, please include as many verbs as you possibly can. And don't forget to <u>underline</u> them. I can't wait to see how the story ends!

_____

_____

_____

_____

_____

_____

How many verbs did you add? Write the number in the box below.

Answers are on page 151.

Wrapping It Up

Chapter Three exploded with action! Here is the "mini-me" version that reminds you what you've learned.

Verbs come in many shapes and sizes, but no matter the shape or size, verbs must agree with their subjects. You have explored action verbs, linking verbs, and helping verbs.

An *action verb* can show action. If, as a writer, you want your readers to <u>jump</u> for joy, try to use action verbs in your writing whenever possible.

A *linking verb* (also known as a *being verb*) expresses a state of being. It connects a subject to a noun in a sentence. Linking verbs are words like *is, are, was, am,* and *were.* They are some form of the verb *be.*

Sometimes a *helping verb* helps the main verb of a sentence. Other times, it stands alone and acts as the main verb. Words like *can, have,* and *may* help the main verb. Words like *are* and *do* can either help the main verb or stand alone.

Verb tense tells you when the action of the verb takes place. There are three main verb tenses: *past, present,* and *future.*

Adverbs give additional information about verbs. Adverbs that tell how something is done often end in the letters *ly,* as in "Shakespeare reads *silently.*"

Let's Hit the Target!
Set #3

<u>Crank</u> up your brain! Let's put your knowledge to use. In the following story, certain words have been underlined. First, read the story. Then, answer the questions in the text boxes about the underlined words.

What a perfect day to visit the water park. All the children were hot, tired, and sweaty. They (1) <u>were</u> ready to cool off and take a break. Shakespeare followed the children to the water park. He (2) <u>loved</u> to watch them splash in the water and scream with delight.

When they reached the water park, the first thing the children decided to do was try out the giant slide. They (3) <u>had</u> heard from their friends that it was the most thrilling part of the water park and were anxious to try it out.

The first person down the slide screamed at the top of his lungs. Shakespeare (4) <u>watched</u> with delight as each of the children tried to see who could be the fastest. Everyone was enjoying the opportunity to splash, go fast, and cool off.

After everyone had a chance to try the slide, the children (5) <u>decided</u> to go to the pool. Several of them tried diving off the high dive. Shakespeare thought that diving was especially

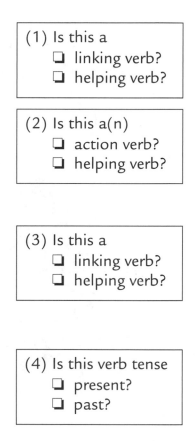

(1) Is this a
- ❑ linking verb?
- ❑ helping verb?

(2) Is this a(n)
- ❑ action verb?
- ❑ helping verb?

(3) Is this a
- ❑ linking verb?
- ❑ helping verb?

(4) Is this verb tense
- ❑ present?
- ❑ past?

(5) Is this verb tense
- ❑ past?
- ❑ present?

exciting. How he wished he did not have feathers so that he could try it, too! He thought to himself, "If only I (6) <u>could</u> jump in right this minute!"

Soon the children (7) <u>were tired</u> and ready to move on to the next event at Grammar World. They all agreed that this was the best trip ever! Shakespeare thought to himself, "It (8) <u>is</u> my job to make sure that the children are enjoying themselves. I (9) <u>am</u> so lucky to live in such a special place." And with that, Shakespeare (10) <u>quickly</u> walked away.

(6) Is this a ❏ linking verb? ❏ helping verb?	
(7) Is this verb tense ❏ past? ❏ present?	
(8) Is this a ❏ linking verb? ❏ helping verb?	
(9) Is this verb tense ❏ past? ❏ present?	
(10) Is this an ❏ adverb? ❏ adjective?	

Answers are on page 151.

Fun Facts—Water Parks

Water parks are as big as summer! But is there more to these watery, winding places than body surfing the day away, riding the swells, and making a splash in the blue waves? Grab your sunscreen and swimsuit, put on your goggles, dive deep, and take a peek.

- Water park safety is more important than anything else. When visiting a water park, always read and follow all park rules. Most injuries are slip-and-fall ones caused by running.

- You know the three R's: reduce, reuse, recycle. Our water supply is precious, and we must do our best to conserve it. In keeping with this goal, many water parks recycle their water through filter systems.

- A water park is a fun way to cool yourself off on a hot day, but it's up to you to protect yourself from the harmful effects of the sun and heat. When visiting a park, be sure to always wear sunscreen and drink plenty of water.

Fun Facts Follow-up
Use your imagination to invent a water ride that will thrill park visitors from coast to coast. Write a descriptive essay about your invention. In your essay, be sure to include the following:

- the design of the ride. (Is it a tube ride that lets you float down a lazy river or is it an eight-lane speed slide where you race against others?)

- the speed of the ride

- the minimum age and height of the rider

- special details about your ride, such as the height of the hills.

Chapter IV

Prepositions, Conjunctions, and Interjections— The Dolphin Show

PREPOSITIONS

The Dolphin Show.

Welcome to the Dolphin Arena where splish-splash sounds abound! Please take a seat and enjoy the show.

Cameras and videotaping are not allowed, but don't worry. This water event is so spectacular that you'll be able to form a lasting picture of it in your mind.

Darla the Darlin' Dolphin will be our first performer. For reasons unknown to us, Darla just so happens to love grammar. Her favorite parts of speech are prepositions. So, *during* her act, Darla will go *over* the pole, *through* the hoop, *into* the water, *beside* the trainer, and *around* the edge *of* the oversized pool *in* five minutes flat. Whew! It took eight prepositions to describe all the movements that Darla will make.

Now that you've seen some prepositions in the sentence about Darla's movements, can you guess what a preposition is or what it does?

A preposition is a word that tells how a noun or pronoun is related to another word in the sentence. It shows time (when), location and direction (where), how, and why.

<u>At</u> noon you will see dolphins jumping <u>in</u> the middle <u>of</u> the pool.

The girl <u>in</u> the pink polka dot bathing suit was chosen to swim <u>with</u> the dolphins.

A preposition is commonly used to give more details about the subject of a sentence. Often prepositions are little words like *to, by, at, in, of,* and *for.*

TRICK TO REMEMBER

To help you identify prepositions, think about Darla the Darlin' Dolphin performing at the water show. Imagine all the movements she makes and how she changes direction: She goes *over* the pole, *through* the hoop, *into* the water, *beside* the trainer, and *around* the edge *of* the oversized pool *in* five minutes flat.

PREPOSITIONAL PHRASES

A prepositional phrase is a group of words that begins with a preposition and ends with a noun or a pronoun called the object of the preposition. The object of the preposition is often the very next word that follows the preposition.

A prepositional phrase can be located at the beginning, middle, or end of a sentence.

Devin sat <u>at the pool</u> to feed the seals <u>on Saturday</u>.

<u>During the water show</u>, Shakespeare took pictures <u>of the walrus</u>.

Sam sat <u>on the diving board at the show</u>.

Sometimes prepositional phrases add detail and *interest* to your writing. Take, for example, the sentence "We went *to Grammar World*." Add a few prepositional phrases to it such as the following: "*Over spring break*, we traveled *by jet to Grammar World in California*."

Other times, prepositional phrases can litter your writing. The following sentence, for example, has too many prepositional phrases in it: *On Saturday,* a bowl *of chocolate ice cream with sprinkles on top* and a cherry *in the middle* melted *on the kitchen counter near the refrigerator.*

Writing is painless! As a writer, you can sprinkle or pour prepositional phrases on the page, but always keep in mind the piece that you're writing. By rereading your work, you will be able to see and hear which parts of your writing piece need more prepositional phrases and which parts need less. You can then revise your writing.

Let's Try It!
Set #21

Find the prepositional phrases in sentences 1 through 8 and underline them. Each sentence has one or more prepositional phrases.

1. On his way to the bus, Aaron saw his friend.

2. The whistle used at the water show was hollow in the middle.

3. The trainer startled the animals when he jumped into the pool.

4. After a day's rest, Lauren went on the field trip with her class.

5. Peter's sunglasses fell behind the bleachers at the dolphin show.

6. On Thursday, the entire school took the bus to Grammar World.

7. In a flash, Cory was ready to line up and leave with the group.

8. Tyler smiled when he saw Shakespeare riding on a dolphin.

Answers are on page 151.

Trick to Remember

A preposition always has an object. An adverb never does.

Treasure Hunt

Hidden in the following story are several prepositional phrases. Can you find them? Draw a box around any prepositional phrases you discover and record the number below.

Tragedy at Grammar World

Tragedy has struck Grammar World! Everyone is in a tizzy! The new baby tiger, Stripes, is missing. He was last seen with his mother during the noon feeding time. The keeper remembers seeing Stripes taking a snooze nestled snugly against his mother.

Oh where, oh where, could Stripes have gone?

How many prepositional phrases did you find? Tally your number in the box below.

☐

Compare the number of prepositional phrases you found with another class member. Do the numbers match?

Complete the story about Stripes, the missing baby tiger. When you are finished writing your story, reread your work and put a box around all the prepositional phrases you have used. I can't wait to see how your story ends!

_____

_____

_____

_____

_____

_____

_____

_____

How many prepositional phrases did you use in your story? Tally your number in the box below.

☐

Answers are on page 152.

CONJUNCTIONS

Conjunctions connect! They join words or groups of words.

Here are examples of conjunctions joining words together:

Riley <u>and</u> Tyler are cousins.

The fourth-grade class enjoyed watching the dolphins <u>and</u> seals perform tricks.

Here are examples of conjunctions joining groups of words:

Flipper couldn't reach the fish <u>because</u> the trainer held it too high.

The walrus will clap its flippers <u>if</u> you call its name.

Here is an entire treasure chest of conjunctions you can use.

and	but	so	for
or	as	because	yet
than	that	until	either
unless	although	however	as

Let's Try It!
Set #22

Find the conjunctions in sentences 1 through 13 and underline them. Happy hunting!

1. Although it was a cloudy day, the fifth-graders were excited about visiting Grammar World.

2. The bus was very crowded, so three students had to sit in each seat.

3. "We're getting as smooshed as pancakes!" yelled Riley and Jennifer.

4. "Please be patient because we are almost there," replied Mrs. Fewell.

5. Finally they arrived at the parking lot and were relieved that the cramped journey was almost over.

6. The students wanted to get off the bus, but Mrs. Fewell reminded them that they had to wait patiently for their turn.

7. Joe and Molly knew that they would be first in line unless Mrs. Fewell said otherwise.

8. They were all excited; yet, they were also packed in like sardines.

9. Finally, Mrs. Fewell gave the signal, and they tumbled off the bus like potatoes falling out of a bag.

10. Because the weather is warm today, I will be able to swim with the dolphins and the whales.

11. I would love to go to the water show with you, but I have already made other plans.

12. We will never visit the water park again unless you agree to go with us.

13. On the Fourth of July, Grammar World is always crowded and noisy.

Answers are on page 152.

Trick to Remember

Some conjunctions are used in pairs.

Both the dolphin and the polar bear are in the water show.

Either you get the popcorn now, or I will get it later.

Conjunction Treasure Hunt

Hidden in the following story are several conjunctions or connecting words. Can you find them? <u>Underline</u> any conjunctions you discover and record your number below. Compare your number of conjunctions with another class member. Do they match?

One steamy August day, herds of people made their way into Grammar World. It seemed as if everyone wanted to keep cool, and what better way to do so than by visiting the refreshing water park?

Within minutes after arriving at Grammar World, children and adults alike were splashing in the pool. Everyone was having a grand old time.

Suddenly, a gigantic whirlpool formed in the pool. The water began to swirl and spin like a tornado. What could be causing this? Was it a faulty drain or a strange windstorm of some sort? Everyone tried to get out of the water, but the current was too strong.

How many conjunctions did you find? Tally your number in the box below.

Now for the really fun part: You get to finish the story. Gosh, I can't wait to see what you write. OK—what happened next? Oh yes, include as many conjunctions as you possibly can and <u>underline</u> them.

_____

_____

_____

_____

_____

_____

_____

_____

Answers are on page 153.

INTERJECTIONS

Zap! Pow! Wow! An interjection is small but mighty!

An interjection is a special word or group of words that expresses a strong feeling such as surprise, excitement, horror, happiness, pain, anger, disgust, or shock.

Hark! An interjection says a lot in a very tiny space. It often stands alone as its own sentence.

Either a comma or an exclamation point comes after an interjection. The information below gives you tips on punctuating interjections.

- Use a *comma* after a mild interjection.

  Gosh, that penguin sure looks funny.

  My goodness, that's a beautiful sundress Alicia is wearing.

- Use an *exclamation point* after an interjection that shows a very strong feeling.

  Yikes! I got drenched at the water show.

  Way to go, Alex!

Careful!

~ Hold your horses! An important thing to know about interjections is not to overuse them in your writing. Otherwise, they will lose their special effects.

Here is an entire treasure chest of interjections you can use.

aha	gosh	whoopee	super	hurray
bravo	ugh	help	well	ouch
oh	oops	good grief	hooray	yeah
hey	yippee	wow	ya-hoo!	yes
phew	yikes	my goodness	yuck	ha

Let's Try It!
Set #23

Find the interjections in the following sentences. Put a circle around all those you find. Happy hunting!

1. "Aha! I have found the missing dolphin whistle," commented Shakespeare.

2. As Portia opened the kettle of dolphin fish treats, she exclaimed, "Phew!"

3. "My goodness," remarked the chaperone as the class walked into the dolphin show.

4. When the show began, Casey yelled, "Hooray!"

5. Karry exclaimed, "Rats! I cannot find a seat at the dolphin show."

Answers are on page 153.

Trick to Remember

You can make up your own interjections to fit your needs.

"Jumpin' horse feathers!" Batman just rode by on the dolphin.

"Great greasy gopher!" The penguin just slipped and fell.

Treasure Hunt

Hidden in the following story are several interjections. Can you find them? <u>Double underline</u> any interjections you discover and record your number below. Remember, conjunctions connect!

When you are finished, compare your number of interjections with another class member. Do they match?

"Hey! Help!" shouted the riders when the Ferris wheel broke down and came to a complete stop.

"Oh, No!" sobbed one rider. "Eeeeeek!"

"Get this ride going!" the others yelled. "Now!"

Suddenly, a child at the very top of the Ferris wheel crawled out of his seat and began to climb down the stalled ride. "Ouch," he exclaimed when one of his fingers scraped a ragged corner of the ride.

"Help! My baby has escaped!" his mother screamed frantically.

"Mad rats! This is certainly a dilemma," thought the operator of the Ferris wheel.

How many interjections did you find? Tally your number in the box below. Compare your answer with a friend's.

Cool beans, Grammar World visitors! Now it's time for the really fun part. You get to finish the story and describe what happened next to those poor riders on the broken-down Ferris wheel. In your story, include as many interjections as you possibly can and <u>double underline</u> them.

I'll be on the edge of my seat waiting to see how your story ends! Hurry up before I fall flat on the floor!

_____

_____

_____

_____

_____

_____

_____

_____

How many interjections did you add? Tally your number in the box below.

☐

Answers are on page 153.

Let's Try It!
Set #24

Find the interjections in the following sentences. <u>Underline</u> them.

1. Yippee! The seal just kissed me on my hand.

2. Gee, this is a breezy day for a trip to the water park.

3. My goodness, I never knew that penguins could be so funny.

4. Wow!

5. Tom exclaimed as he stepped on the gum, "Yuck!"

6. After the dolphin show the entire audience yelled, "Bravo!"

Answers are on page 154.

Let's Try It—Supersized!
Set #25

Show what you know about prepositions, prepositional phrases, conjunctions, and interjections by doing what is asked in each section.

Underline the preposition in sentences 1 through 13.

1. The turtle was hiding under the rock.

2. Please go around the Water Show Building and meet me at the New Wave Aquarium.

3. We will go home after the last dolphin show.

4. You may sit by Aaron on the bus.

5. Your backpack is under the seat of the bus.

Put a box around the prepositional phrases below.

6. Joe wanted to pat the penguin on its head.

7. During the night, the trainer fed the animals.

8. Our class cheered when we were chosen to see the water show under the bridge.

9. Shakespeare sat under the diving board at the dolphin show.

Circle the conjunction in each sentence.

10. Alex and Casey were picked to feed fish to the polar bears and penguins.

11. The sleepy students arrived home from the field trip and went straight to bed.

12. Josh and Christine couldn't wait to get to the park because they had front-row seats at the water show.

13. I want to snack on either popcorn or peanuts at the show.

For sentences 14 through 17, put a box around the interjections you find.

14. Good grief! I am soaked from being splashed by the whale.

15. Yikes! I knew we would have a fabulous time.

16. Cool beans! The rides at Grammar World are out of this world.

17. The crowd screamed, "Stop!"

Answers are on page 154.

Let's Try It (Mixed Review)!
Set #26

Sharpen your pencil. It's GO time. Show all that you know by doing what is asked.

Underline the prepositions in the following sentences.

1. After the water show, Kelsey got a chance to pet a dolphin in the tank.

2. He climbed up the stairs and ran quickly to the tank.

3. A huge smile appeared on his face as he touched the dolphin's smooth skin.

4. On Saturday, Peter traveled with the band to Grammar World.

Draw a box around the prepositional phrases.

5. After the field trip, Lauren skipped to the bus, fell on the stairs, and skinned the top of her knee.

6. Her teacher found a special Scooby Doo Band-Aid to put on her scraped knee.

7. Lauren wrote a thank-you note to her teacher.

8. Whether you're at school or on a field trip, it's nice to have a caring teacher.

Draw <u>two lines</u> under each conjunction and <u>a dashed line</u> under each interjection.

9. "Yikes!" Devin yelled, when the water splashed out of the tank during the dolphin show.

10. Tim and Todd were so excited at the dolphin show that they screamed "Whoopee" after every trick.

Answers are on page 154.

BONUS SECTION: PREPOSITIONS

Now that you are becoming an expert at identifying prepositions, it's time to search for some in the books you read.

Go to your social studies book and find three sentences that contain prepositions. Remember to begin each sentence with a capital letter and end each sentence with the correct end mark.

1. _____

_____

2. _____

_____

3. _____

_____

Go to a newspaper or magazine and find three interesting sentences that contain prepositions. Write the sentences below and then box the prepositions. Share your choices with a friend or classmate.

1. _____

_____

_____

2. _____

_____

_____

3. _____

_____

_____

BONUS SECTION: PREPOSITIONAL PHRASES

What book are you currently reading? Is it a mystery like *The Gadget* by Paul Zindel? Perhaps it's one of the *Series of Unfortunate Events* by Lemony Snicket (curses, Count Olaf!). Maybe you prefer fantasies like *Runaway Ralph* by Beverly Cleary.

Dig into the book that you're reading and find examples of prepositional phrases. Write your examples below. Choose interesting ones that the rest of the class would like to hear about.

Write the sentences below and then underline each prepositional phrase.

1. _____

_____

_____

2. _____

_____

_____

3. _____

_____

_____

Bonus Section: Conjunctions

We use conjunctions every day in a thousand different ways.

Bring an empty cereal box from home to school. (If you forget to empty it, you can eat the cereal on your way to school!)

List below all the sentences or phrases on the cereal box that contain a conjunction.

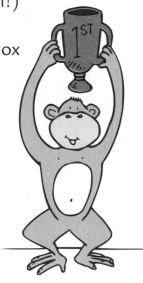

Be ready to share your discoveries with the class. You might even have a contest to determine which cereal box contains the most conjunctions. (Don't worry, conjunctions are sugar-free!)

Write the sentences or phrases below and circle each conjunction.

1. _____

_____

_____

2. _____

_____

_____

3. _____

_____

_____

BONUS SECTION: INTERJECTIONS

Good grief! There are certainly a lot of interjections in the newspaper. If you don't believe me, see for yourself. Search through a newspaper to find examples of interjections. Gosh! I am sure you will be surprised at how many you will discover.

Write the interjections below. Now!

1. _____

2. _____

3. _____

4. _____

5. _____

6. _____

7. _____

Wow! For extra credit, keep going and list more interjections here!

1. _____

2. _____

3. _____

4. _____

Wrapping It Up

Good for you! You've become an expert on prepositions, conjunctions, and interjections.

A preposition comes before a noun or pronoun. It is often a little word like *of*, *in*, or *to*.

Conjunctions connect! They join words or groups of words. They are words like *but*, *and*, *so*, *because*, *or*, *unless*, and *however*.

Interjections are special words or groups of words that show surprise, excitement, upset, or shock. Experts like you choose their interjections wisely. They know that using too many interjections in their writing can weaken their effects.

Let's Hit the Target!

Set #4

In the short story below, you will find prepositions, prepositional phrases, conjunctions, and interjections. First read through the whole story. Then reread it and answer the questions in the text boxes that refer to the underlined words.

It was no secret that Shakespeare loved the dolphin show. He was fascinated at how graceful (1) <u>and</u> powerful these mammals are.

(1) Is this a
❏ conjunction?
❏ preposition?

It always thrilled him to see them leap (2) <u>through</u> hoops held high in the air.

(3) <u>"Wow!"</u> he thought as the trainer put all the dolphins through their paces. Shakespeare was amazed when two dolphins jumped (4) <u>through a giant hoop</u> at the same time.

Suddenly, the crowd became completely silent. All the lights were turned off and a drum roll could be heard. Like a giant water bomb, three beautiful dolphins sprang out (5) <u>of the pool</u> at exactly the same time. (6) <u>"Ahhh!"</u> the crowd yelled. The three dolphins jumped through a giant hoop of fire. The crowd roared.

All too soon, the dolphin show came to a close. The crowd began to leave. It had been an amazing display of talent and beauty. Everyone agreed that the dolphin show was terrific! "(7) <u>Bravo!</u>" exclaimed Shakespeare as he walked outside with the children.

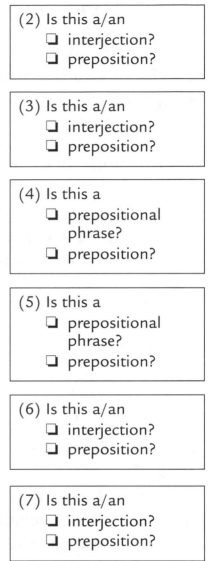

(2) Is this a/an
- ❏ interjection?
- ❏ preposition?

(3) Is this a/an
- ❏ interjection?
- ❏ preposition?

(4) Is this a
- ❏ prepositional phrase?
- ❏ preposition?

(5) Is this a
- ❏ prepositional phrase?
- ❏ preposition?

(6) Is this a/an
- ❏ interjection?
- ❏ preposition?

(7) Is this a/an
- ❏ interjection?
- ❏ preposition?

Answers are on page 155.

CALLING ALL DOLPHIN FANS! Now it's time to swim to the story center at Dolphin Cove and read a whale of a tale. After you've read the story, reread it and notice how conjunctions, interjections, prepositions, and prepositional phrases make the story colorful and exciting.

A Day to Remember

Shea and Adrianna had front-row seats at the dolphin show and were waiting patiently for the performance to begin.

The lights dimmed. There was a drum roll. Suddenly, three dolphins sprang from the pool of sparkling water at the same time and flipped in the air. The entire arena filled with screams of delight.

A booming voice coming from the loudspeaker announced that the Preposition Show! was ready to begin. The crowd was told that the dolphins would be jumping over, under, around, through, beside, and beneath the colorful hoops that were being held up for all to see. Adrianna and Shea couldn't believe how talented these amazing animals were. My goodness! They understood everything said to them and reacted perfectly. Amazing!

Shea was especially impressed with the show. She had spent hours over the past month learning about dolphins. She knew that dolphins, like you and me, are mammals. They have teeth, a little hair, and a four-chambered heart. They nurse their young.

Shea had learned many interesting fun facts about dolphins. Here are some of them. The dolphin's tail is called its flukes. The biggest dolphin is the killer whale. Killer whale calves are about 8 feet long at birth and can grow to more than 20 feet long. Bottlenose dolphins are about 3½ feet long at birth and grow to 8 or 9 feet long. Dolphins eat a variety of fish and squid. A dolphin's cone-shaped teeth interlock to catch fish. Their teeth are not used to chew, and they swallow their food whole. Shea whispered these facts to Adrianna as they watched the show with wonder.

When the show was about halfway over, a loud trumpet sounded, Da! Da! and a female voice announced that some lucky audience member was about to be chosen to be in the show and feed the dolphins. Shea held her breath as the lucky ticket number was read, "4022269." She was nervous to see what her ticket number was but managed to squeeze her eyes open to just a slit. Her heart sank as she read the number on her ticket— "4022268." Oh my gosh! Shea had missed the lucky number by just one digit! Tears welled up in her eyes, and she started to cry. She had hoped and dreamed of this moment. She had come so close to having her wish come true. She had missed it by just one tiny little number!

Suddenly, she felt a second ticket being placed into her hand. She glanced at her sister.

Adrianna tucked her ticket into Shea's hand. Shea didn't even have to look at the number. She just knew it was a match! Yes! Adrianna had gotten the winning ticket and was giving it to her little sister. Now, Shea really began to cry.

Before she knew what was happening, Adrianna pushed Shea onto the stage and the show began! The dolphin trainer told Shea how to stand and hold the fish so that the dolphin would be able to snatch it from her hand. Everything happened so quickly. Before Shea knew it there she was, standing before the entire audience and feeding the dolphins. Amazing! Adrianna clapped until her hands tingled and turned bright red. This was a day that both girls would remember forever.

Adrianna and Shea left the dolphin show at Grammar World with huge smiles on their faces. One of Shea's most special dreams had come true. She had gotten to feed a dolphin. She had been close enough to one of these adorable creatures to look it right in the eye. Because Shea had researched dolphins and knew how smart they are, she was sure that the dolphin knew how much she cared.

For Adrianna, it had been joy enough just to watch her little sister's beaming face. Adrianna knew Shea would not be able to sleep that night when they returned home.

Evening had come. The sun was setting at Grammar World. The light was fading. It had truly been an remarkable day for both girls. From the train ride in the morning, to the rides, to the water park, and finally to the dolphin show, it had been a day to remember.

As the girls made their way to the bleachers where they would watch the fireworks, Adrianna thought she saw something moving in the bushes. She thought that it was the same silly chicken she had seen earlier in the day—the same chicken who had been in her dream the night before. But how could that be? "I think I am going crazy!" Adrianna said to herself. "How could I be seeing a chicken all over Grammar World? It doesn't make sense!" She was just about to mention it to Shea when both girls heard a loud BOOM! The fireworks were about to begin. The girls rushed to find good seats before the show began.

Shakespeare just chuckled to himself as he settled in to watch the show.

Fun Facts—Dolphins

- There is something about dolphins that makes kids and grown-ups happy.

- Scientists don't know a lot about the lives of dolphins in the ocean, but they're trying to learn.

- Dolphins are mammals, not fish. They breathe air using lungs, just like you do.

- There are about 30 to 40 kinds of dolphins, such as bottlenose dolphins and orcas. Some species like the Indus River dolphin are listed as endangered.

- Dolphins have a layer of blubber (fat) that protects them from the cold.

- Every dolphin has its own special whistle that makes it different from other dolphins, just like a human fingerprint.

- Dolphins eat fish, squid, and shrimp. They do not chew their food but swallow it whole.

Fun Facts Follow-up

For a whale of a good time, complete one or more of the following activities.

- Dolphins are members of the whale family. Use the library and internet to research fun facts about whales and write a mini-report about them. Or, if you prefer, you can write a mini-report on another sea creature like the porpoise.

- Write a letter to the local newspaper about whether sea animals like dolphins should be kept in captivity or set free. In your letter, be sure to explain your opinion fully and try to convince readers to feel the same way that you do.

Shakespeare hopes that you'll have loads of fun writing about marine animals. He knows that you'll apply the great grammar skills you've learned at Grammar World to create a writing piece that will make a splash!

Chapter V

Mechanics and Other Stuff—
The Fireworks

Boom! Boom! Boom!

Mechanics are like the fireworks show at a theme park. Often they come at the very end and serve as a finale. Other times, they are inserted here and there to add meaning and color, like a sparkler. Mechanics are necessary to help us communicate clearly and correctly. Without mechanics, we would not know where the bang-boom occurs in the text.

PUNCTUATION

Punctuation marks are like traffic signals. They tell you when to start, stop, slow down, and listen.

PERIODS

A period is one of the stop signs of punctuation.

Use a period

- at the end of a sentence that states a fact or gives an order.

    Joe couldn't wait for the fireworks. (fact)

    Kelly, please be quiet. (order)

- after initials

    C. S. Lewis

    M. C. Higgens, the Great

- after abbreviations

    Mr. Mrs. Ms. Dr.

COMMAS

When you see a comma in a sentence, take a breath and pause.

While waiting for the fireworks display, the children watched a clown juggle oranges and bananas.

Use a comma

- between a city and state

    Greenfield, Indiana

- following the greeting in a friendly letter

    Dear John,

- to set off a direct quotation

    "Look at the amazing fireworks display," remarked Lindsay.

- before *and*, before *but*, or to make a compound sentence.

    The show began with a parade of sparklers, and it ended with bottle rockets.

- to separate three or more items in a series

We ate hot dogs, hamburgers, and French fries before the fireworks lit up the sky.

- with nouns in a direct address

    Kathy, please bring a bucket of water for the fireworks.

- after introductory phrases in a sentence

    No, the clouds of smoke do not bother me.

COLONS

Use a colon

- after the greeting in a business letter

  Dear Mr. Bigstuff:

- to show that a list is following

  The items needed for the recipe include: eggs, butter, and flour

CAPITALIZATION

Be sure to use capital letters for the following:

- proper nouns and initials in names, and proper adjectives

  George W. Bush, American

- the first word in a sentence

  Tom ran home with the great news.

- the first word in a direct quotation

  Shawn yelled, "Put the fire out!"

- the greeting of a letter

  Dear Joan,

- the first word in the closing of a letter

  Yours truly,

- the pronoun I

  When can I have a turn?

- cities, states, countries, continents

  McCordsville, Indiana, U.S.A, North America

- geographic names like bodies of water, landforms, roads, and buildings

  the Atlantic Ocean, the Rocky Mountains, Route 66, the White House

- names of languages and religions

  English, Methodist

- words as names

  Uncle George, Mama

- days of the week, months, holidays

  Monday, April, Christmas

- business names

  American Eagle, Kroger

- titles used with a name

  Dr. Tom O'Conner, Senator Beverly Gard

ABBREVIATIONS

- Titles and names

    Mister—Mr.   *Senator—Sen.*

- Days of the week

    Monday—Mon.   *Friday—Fri.*

    Tuesday—Tues.   *Saturday—Sat.*

    Wednesday—Wed.   *Sunday—Sun.*

    Thursday—Thurs.

- Months

    January—Jan.   *July—July*

    February—Feb.   *August—Aug.*

    March—Mar.   *September—Sept.*

    April—Apr.   *October—Oct.*

    May—May   *November—Nov.*

    June—June   *December—Dec.*

- Addresses

Drive—Dr.	*Street—St.*
Avenue—Ave.	*Boulevard—Blvd.*
Lane—Ln.	*Post Office—P.O.*

- States

  The United States Postal System calls for each state to have a two-letter abbreviation with no period at the end.

Let's Hit the Target!
Set #5

Let's put your knowledge of capitalization and punctuation to use. Read the short story below. Then answer the questions in the text boxes.

As the day ended and the sun began to set, Shakespeare made his way to the grandstand to watch the fireworks show (1) This was certainly one of his favorite times of the day. (2) as the children and their families began to arrive, the loudspeaker announced that the fireworks show would begin in ten minutes. (3) Hooray!" shouted the crowd (4) Suddenly a loud explosion was heard. Everyone was silent. Had the fireworks

(1) What is missing?
- ❑ a period
- ❑ a question mark

(2) What is missing?
- ❑ a capital letter
- ❑ No correction is needed.

(3) What is missing?
- ❑ quotation marks
- ❑ No correction is needed.

(4) What is missing?
- ❑ a period
- ❑ an exclamation mark

already begun (5) To everyone's surprise, (6) shakespeare stepped onto the stage.

(5) What is missing?
❑ a period
❑ a question mark

"Dont (7) panic. There is nothing to be afraid of. One of the fireworks boxes was placed too close to a candle and it blew up. No one was near, and no one was hurt. Now let's get this fireworks show started!"

(6) What is missing?
❑ a capital letter
❑ No correction is needed.

The crowd cheered as the show began, and the sky took on all the colors of the rainbow.

(7) What is missing?
❑ an apostrophe
❑ a comma

Answers are on page 156.

Boom! Crash! Bam! The sky was filled with brilliant colors and exploding sounds as the fireworks show at Grammar World began. Adrianna and Shea watched with awe as the glittery colors filled the ceiling of the world. The crowd "oohed" and "aaahed" as each new firework transformed the night sky into daylight.

All too soon, the grand finale firework appeared in the air. It was an American flag with thousands of stars bursting around it. As the last stars of the fireworks twinkled out, Adrianna and Shea knew that their day at Grammar World was over. How they hated to leave!

Their parents had planned to pick them up at the gate around nine o'clock, and that left the girls very little time to squander. As they rushed to find their way to the gates, they glanced up at the gigantic Grammar World sign and saw a chicken winking and waving good-bye to them. The girls were astonished. They waved back, and the chicken winked at them. Immediately, both girls said at the very same time, "It's him!" Quickly, they shared with each other the dreams they had had the night before and talked about all the times that they had seen the chicken throughout the day. They both agreed it was as if he had been watching over them, making sure that they were safe and enjoying themselves.

The girls burst into laughter thinking about how amazing it was that they had both seen this curious creature. They glanced back up at the Grammar World sign, hoping for some explanation, but the silly chicken had vanished. Had the entire thing been a figment of their imaginations? Had he ever existed?

Suddenly, they realized the time and knew they must hurry. Gosh, they surely didn't want to leave without solving the mystery, but they had no choice.

As they exited the gates of Grammar World, the girls took one last look back at the magical theme park. And, guess who they saw waving to them from the gate? The girls burst into laughter. They agreed that this had been the very best day of their lives! "Grammar World rocks!" they thought to themselves.

Seated in the back seat of their parents' car, Adrianna and Shea were still talking about their amazing day at Grammar World. What had been their favorite part of the visit? Was it the ride on the express train that let them see the entire park? Was it the rides on which they had screamed their lungs out with excitement? Was it the water park where they got soaking wet, half the time on purpose? Was it the dolphin show where Shea held the fish in her hand for the dolphin to eat? Maybe it was the fireworks show at the end of the day when they watched colorful fireworks roar across the sky. All in all, it had been one of the very best days of their lives.

Just as they were drifting off to sleep, they remembered the chicken that they had seen all over Grammar World.

"What do you suppose it all means?"
Adrianna asked Shea. There was no response.
Shea was fast asleep. Soon, Adrianna was,
too.

Fun Facts—Fireworks

- Fireworks originated in China about 2,000 years ago.

- Queen Elizabeth I of Great Britain loved watching fireworks so much that she created the position of "Fire Master of England."

- William Shakespeare, one of the greatest writers of all time, mentions fireworks in his writings. Grammar World's very own Shakespeare is named after William Shakespeare.

- Most of us enjoy the excitement of a fireworks display. The same is not true for pets. Because animals tend to have sharp hearing, the loud noise of firecrackers can hurt their ears and cause them pain. Pets should be kept indoors when fireworks are being launched.

- The most important thing to remember about firecrackers is safety. Fireworks can be very dangerous if not used properly. Accidents involving fireworks happen yearly.

- Only grown-ups should touch fireworks. Fireworks safety rules must always be followed.

Chapter VI

Putting It All Together

Let's go around the park one more time, with gusto! We'll take another look at all that Grammar World has to offer, and we'll do it through poetry.

A Play Land of Words

From a stomach-churning, screeching ride
To a gentle, quieter one
Grammar World is bursting with fun!

Vivid *verbs* giving nouns something to do
Slide, ride, dash, splash
Grammar World is the theme park for you!

Adjectives describing nouns
Funny, colorful, playful clowns.

Zap! Pow! Wow! Interjections surely do yell
Expressing emotions very well.

Pronouns parade merrily
Shakespeare becoming *him or he*
You and Shakespeare becoming *we*.

Adverbs are bossy, that's nothing new
Telling verbs, adverbs, and adjectives what to do.
Telling them how, how much, and when
Slowly, very, yesterday, then.

Prepositional phrases dress up your writing
And sometimes make it more exciting.
Through the barnyard, under the tree
In Grammar World, that's where Shakespeare will be.

Conjunctions link in so many ways
As in mosquito-ridden nights *and* buggy days.

Unplanned *fragments* are not cool or neat
Use a *subject* and *predicate* to make your *sentence complete*.

But of all the grammar in Play Land,
Shakespeare must admit
Vivid *verbs* are his absolute favorite!
He loves to *zip* down chutes with water *spraying*.
And *squawk* at tigers *pouncing* and *playing*.

Shakespeare and the entire crew at Grammar World hope that you've had a mega-thrilling journey through the park. Now, they want to give you the chance to show your stuff and put your brain to good use.

Let's Hit the Target!
Set #6

In the following story, certain groups of words have been underlined. Answer the questions that go along with each of the underlined words.

It was a dark and stormy night. The gates at Grammar World (1) <u>had closed</u> and everyone had gone home for the evening. At least everyone was supposed to have already left. The theme park should have been deserted.

(2) <u>The</u> train was parked (3) <u>at the station</u> and everything seemed normal. But something was wrong. What was it?

The dolphins were resting (4) <u>quietly</u> in their tank. Only the gentle swishing of the water as they swam silently by could be heard. (5) <u>The trainers</u> had gone home hours ago, (6) <u>and</u> everything was safely locked up—or was it?

All the water at the water park had been shut off for the day. The (7) <u>blue</u> slide glistened as clouds passed by the moon every now and then.

(8) <u>A</u> storm was about to hit Grammar World. The wind began to howl. "Oooooowwwwooo," it (9) <u>moaned</u> through the trees.

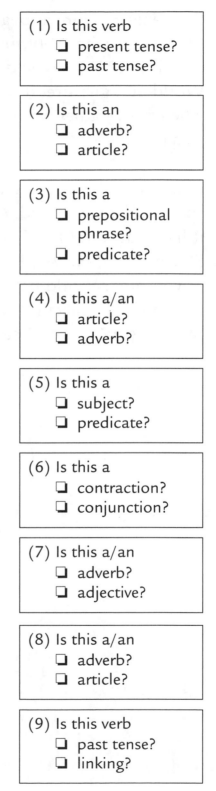

(1) Is this verb
- ❑ present tense?
- ❑ past tense?

(2) Is this an
- ❑ adverb?
- ❑ article?

(3) Is this a
- ❑ prepositional phrase?
- ❑ predicate?

(4) Is this a/an
- ❑ article?
- ❑ adverb?

(5) Is this a
- ❑ subject?
- ❑ predicate?

(6) Is this a
- ❑ contraction?
- ❑ conjunction?

(7) Is this a/an
- ❑ adverb?
- ❑ adjective?

(8) Is this a/an
- ❑ adverb?
- ❑ article?

(9) Is this verb
- ❑ past tense?
- ❑ linking?

Suddenly, a figure appeared in the shadows. (10) <u>It</u> was small, but moved quickly. What could it be? Who would be at Grammar World at night after it had shut down and when the weather was so stormy? Who (11) <u>was</u> it?

From behind a (12) <u>dark</u> wall came a short, spry bird of some kind. At least it looked as if it had feathers. (13) Good grief! It was Shakespeare! He was just taking one last look at Grammar World before turning in for the evening. That silly bird scared me! Goodnight, Shakespeare. Sweet dreams!

Answers are on page 156.

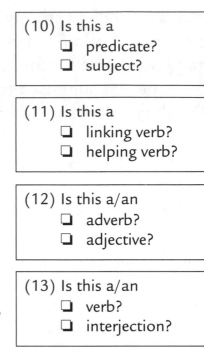

(10) Is this a
- ❏ predicate?
- ❏ subject?

(11) Is this a
- ❏ linking verb?
- ❏ helping verb?

(12) Is this a/an
- ❏ adverb?
- ❏ adjective?

(13) Is this a/an
- ❏ verb?
- ❏ interjection?

Answer Key

CHAPTER I

Answers to Let's Try It! Set #1
page 4

1. Kelsey applauded as the ringmaster blew his whistle. (declarative)

2. Why did Riley arrive so late? (interrogative)

3. Have you seen the white tiger act? (interrogative)

4. Tom wanted to sit by his best friend during the Animal Magic Show. (declarative)

5. The rain poured on the cheering train riders. (declarative)

6. Libby wanted to feed the monkeys. (declarative)

7. When can we visit the petting zoo? (interrogative)

8. Where in the world is Shakespeare? (interrogative)

9. Once upon a time in a magical theme park not so far away, there was a jungle full of amazing animals. (declarative)

10. Even after a long day at Grammar World, Tim did not want to leave. (declarative)

Answers to Let's Try It! Set #2
page 6

1. Meet me at the wooden roller coaster after lunch. (command)

2. Watch out! (command)

3. What a magical day! (exclamation)

4. Go to the middle of the park. (command)

5. Grammar World is the best place to learn! (exclamation)

6. Take the Play Land express train. (command)

7. Look out below! (command)

8. Please help your sister find her heart necklace. (command)

9. Come home before it gets dark. (command)

10. Yes! (exclamation)

Answers to Let's Try It! Set #3
page 9

1. <u>The students in Mr. Larsen's class</u> <u>gave each other high five's when they won free tickets to see the dancing bear show.</u>

2. <u>Peter and Tyler</u> <u>played in the Grammar World All-Star Band.</u>

3. <u>The sun</u> <u>smiled on the playful children.</u>

4. <u>Molly</u> <u>fixed the stage for the performance.</u>

5. <u>Four kittens</u> <u>were born on Saturday.</u>

6. <u>Shakespeare</u> <u>sang the children's favorite song.</u>

7. <u>Tim and Todd</u> <u>played football at the dome.</u>

8. <u>Libby</u> <u>will ride the monorail to get to the other side of the park.</u>

9. <u>Black clouds</u> <u>filled the sky before the storm.</u>

10. <u>The third-graders</u> <u>won the contest at the water park.</u>

Answers to Let's Try It! Set #4
page 11

Here are some sample answers. Other answers are possible.

1. The bus driver and many of the children were sunburned.

2. Scott and Lauren ate pizza for lunch.

3. Tim and Todd waited patiently for the afternoon parade.

4. Ariel and Sam wore comfortable sneakers to Grammar World.

5. Lauren and Tracy enjoyed a long nature walk.

6. <u>Shakespeare and the children</u> saw an animal puppet show.

7. <u>Dillon and Lindsay</u> ate breakfast with their favorite characters.

8. <u>Saturday and Sunday</u> were the busiest days to visit the park.

9. <u>Mr. Katz and Ms. Leon</u> chaperoned the field trip.

10. <u>All the children and their parents</u> stopped for lemonade and honey-dipped pretzels.

Answers to Let's Try It! Set #5
page 14

1. Alex licked his fingers after eating the tasty brownie and washed his hands.

2. Peter strolled through the animal gallery at Grammar World and admired the colorful posters and photographs.

3. The animals at Grammar World jump for joy when children arrive at the theme park but feel down in the dumps when the children leave.

4. The polite children <u>picked</u> up litter on the ground at Grammar World and <u>threw</u> it in a nearby trash can.

5. Shakespeare <u>thanked</u> the children for helping to keep the theme park clean and <u>gave</u> them cuddly stuffed teddy bears for their efforts.

6. The children <u>were proud</u> of themselves for what they had done and <u>promised</u> to always respect the environment.

7. Cory <u>went</u> to the art corner and <u>made</u> a poster about our environment and the precious animals that live in it.

8. Joe <u>believes</u> that Grammar World treats the animals that live there kindly and <u>hopes</u> that other theme parks and zoos do as well.

Answers to Let's Try It! Set #6
page 16

Here are some sample answers. Other answers are possible.

1. Billy wanted to see the different areas in Grammar World, but Laura wanted to stay in the water safari area.

2. Scooter explored all areas of the animal kingdom, but Riley spent the entire afternoon with Reptile Rob and his buddies.

3. Rita rode the train in the early morning, and Daniel rode it late in the evening.

4. The students didn't want to leave the park at dusk, so they stayed until midnight.

5. The train slid into the noisy depot, and it screeched as it came to a sudden stop.

6. Five cars were added to the train at the end of the day, and a new engine was added the following night.

7. Casey wants to go to the water park now, but Molly will go after the parade.

8. Aaron visited Grammar World in the spring, and he plans to return in the fall.

9. Joe ran to the concession stand, but Lauren remained seated.

10. Lions and tigers were loaded aboard the train, but the bears were left behind. (Oh my!)

11. We were ready to see the rest of Grammar World, but Sabrina wanted to play with the animals a little longer.

12. The students were going to trek into the forest, so they wore comfortable footwear.

Answers to Let's Try It! Set #7
page 20

Many answers are possible. Here are some sample ones.

1. <u>Peter</u> came face to face with an elephant.

2. <u>Shari</u> grinned when she saw the parade of tropical fish.

3. When I met Shakespeare, he <u>**squawked with delight**</u>.

4. After the torrential downpour, the students were <u>**soaked**</u>.

5. <u>Keith</u> whistled while he peeled the bubble gum off his shoe.

6. <u>**The fifth-graders**</u> made the audience giggle.

7. Seventy-five barrels of chicken feed

   Correction: Seventy-five barrels of chicken feed

arrived at Grammar World, much to Shakespeare's delight.

8. Flash photography is

   Correction: Flash photography is not allowed because it can frighten the animals.

9. The underwater hippo viewing area was amazing.

   No correction: This is a complete sentence.

10. When you trek into the forest

    Correction: When you trek into the forest, you will have face-to-face encounters with all kinds of wild animals.

11. eye contact with a tiger

    Correction: I can't wait to tell my friends that I made eye contact with a tiger.

12. hundreds of wild, exotic, and rare animals

    Correction: Hundreds of wild, exotic, and rare animals call Grammar World their home.

    Another possible correction: At Grammar World, you will see hundreds of wild, exotic, and rare animals.

13. didn't feel so hot when they got off the safari bus

    Correction: Two grown-ups didn't feel so hot when they got off the safari bus.

Answers to Let's Try It! Set #8
page 22

1. *Sample answer:* Lauren wore a neon-green, stuffed snake around her neck. She could be seen from a mile away.

   Sample answer: Lauren wore a neon-green, stuffed snake around her neck so that she could be seen from a mile away.

2. On the way home we had a flat tire, but Haley fixed it.

3. *Sample answer:* After a fun-filled day at Grammar World, the children were tired and fell asleep quickly.

   Sample answer: After a fun-filled day at Grammar World, the children were tired. They fell asleep quickly.

4. *Sample answer:* Shakespeare watched all the children arrive every morning. He

liked to wave to them as they entered Grammar World.

Sample answer: Shakespeare watched all the children arrive every morning because he liked to wave to them as they entered Grammar World.

5. A loud noise exploded. The fireworks were about to begin.

6. The train's whistle sounded like a bell, a gong, and a scream.

7. Clay and Cindy knew where all the rest stops were.

Answers to Let's Try It— Supersized! Set #9 *page 23*

Many answers are possible.

1. *Sample answer:* Steven likes to visit the bear and monkey exhibits.

2. *Sample answer:* On Saturday, Mike and I went to the Wildlife Theatre. We saw elephant shows.

   Sample answer: On Saturday, Mike and I went to the Wildlife Theatre and saw elephant shows.

3. *This is already a complete sentence.*

4. *Sample answer:* This may sound strange, but Shakespeare knows how to soar like a bald eagle!

Answers to Let's Hit the Target! Set #1 *page 25*

1. statement
2. exclamation
3. command
4. exclamation
5. statement
6. subject
7. predicate
8. run-on
9. fragment
10. compound predicate
11. compound subject

CHAPTER II

Answers to Let's Try It! Set #10 *page 36*

1. the **student's** water bottle
2. the **baby's** rattle
3. the **dog's** bone
4. the **actor's** script

5. the **elephant's** trunk

6. the **snail's** slime

7. the **snake's** fang

8. the **deer's** horns

9. the **women's** laughter

10. the **teams'** footballs

11. the **birds'** whistles

12. the **swimmers'** skis

13. the **moose's** antlers

14. the **children's** favorite rides

15. the **riders'** tickets

Answers to Let's Try It! Set #11
page 39

1. <u>I</u> rode the Shakespeare Skyscraper after the sun went down.

2. <u>You</u> can go to Grammar World with us next week.

3. <u>We</u> will take five buses on the field trip.

4. <u>They</u> want to play football at Grammar World.

5. <u>It</u> is the first day of spring.

6. <u>She</u> is one of the funniest clowns.

7. <u>He</u> will visit Grammar World during his spring break next year.

8. <u>They</u> saw Shakespeare eating a foot-long hot dog on the Ferris wheel.

9. **They** will have to buy tickets for the ride.

10. **They** had a terrific time.

11. **They** rode the alligator ride until after dark.

12. **He** will return soon.

13. **They** couldn't believe their eyes.

14. **He** loved seeing the smiles on *their* faces.

15. **It** was happy when it found bits of hot dog and potato chips around the trash barrel.

Answers to Let's Try It! Set #12
page 42

1. Isabella ran away from <u>us</u>.

2. The monkey will throw the peanut to <u>him</u>.

3. All the performers sang to <u>us</u>.

4. Shakespeare found the right answer on the test and drew an orange circle around <u>it</u>.

5. Please give the big, green ball to <u>me</u> so that we can play water polo.

6. Shea told Adrianna to give the ball to <u>her</u>.

7. The clown ran to Tracy and <u>me</u>.

8. Kelsey gave the cotton candy to <u>her</u>.

9. The monkey ran to Shakespeare and <u>him</u>.

10. Molly wanted the Frisbee, so Casey threw it to <u>her</u>.

11. When the clowns walked by, we laughed at <u>them</u>.

12. Keith saw Lauren and gave his ticket to <u>her</u>.

Answers to Let's Try It! Set #13
page 45

1. Kathy stood in line for <u>her</u> favorite ride.

2. Caroline liked <u>her</u> movie-star sunglasses that she had bought at Grammar World.

3. At dark, Peter saw <u>his</u> best friend.

4. Shakespeare wiped the paint from <u>his</u> white feathers.

5. Don't chew with <u>your</u> mouth open!

6. We did not know where <u>our</u> class was going.

Answers to Let's Try It! Set # 14
page 48

1. Little Riley cried when the tiny, yellow toy boats floated past him.

2. The beautiful full moon shone on Grammar World at midnight.

3. Last Saturday, Molly decided to visit the haunted castle.

4. Five students screamed as the fantastic blue bus flew by.

5. Shakespeare painted beautiful, bright numbers on all the new bumper cars.

6. When she was in the scary fun house, Shea came face to face with a large make-believe bat.

7. One happy girl will ride the fast roller coaster.

8. Nervous (students) laughed during the dark (part) of the scary (ride)

9. Blue (dolphins) swam around the sloppy log (ride)

10. A funny animal (movie) was shown at Grammar World.

11. The hilarious (play) was about goofy (animals) of all shapes and sizes.

12. We saw purple popping (penguins,) yellow yawning (yaks,) and silvery slimy (snakes.)

Answers to Let's Try It! Set #15
page 50

1. Grammar World was busy with happy visitors.

2. The purple grape slurpie was refreshing to the hot, exhausted child.

3. The haunted castle was filled with screaming people.

4. The fifth-grade students were thrilled to be riding such incredible rides.

5. Sandy decided to visit the concession stand to buy a yummy funnel cake.

6. The moon was red and glowing at night.

7. The summer weather was unpredictable.

8. His large, black hat is missing.

9. Her cherry cola was frosty and refreshing.

10. Todd saw a gray mouse running through the dark fun house.

Answers to Let's Try It! Set #16
page 52

1. The Grammar Gremlin is **more** fun to ride than the swings.

2. Adrianna was the **most** tired of all the children.

3. Shakespeare is **more** friendly than his barnyard buddies.

4. Lindsay ate **more** bubble gum ice cream than Tim.

5. Todd ate the **most** ice cream of all.

6. Grammar World is **more** entertaining than other theme parks.

7. Devin is the **most** impressive cheerleader.

8. Our city's parks are the **most** beautiful in the state.

Answers to Let's Try It! Set #17
page 55

1. Scott said that **he'd** go to Grammar Canyon with me.

2. **I'm** not afraid of heights, so let's go on the swing ride.

3. **She's** feeling dizzy.

4. **He'll** buy an all-season pass to Grammar World.

5. **Don't** be surprised if Shakespeare shows up.

Answers to Let's Hit the Target! Set #2 *page 56*

1. proper noun (Shakespeare)

2. common noun (crash)

3. plural noun (children)

4. pronoun (They)

5. subject pronoun (I)

6. object pronoun (them)

7. common noun (equipment)

8. subject pronoun (She)

9. proper noun (Ferris wheel)

10. article (a)

11. adjective (happiest)

12. contraction (can't)

CHAPTER III

Answers to Let's Try It! Set #18
page 69

1. Lauren **hopped** across the road to reach the other side.

2. Peter **slapped** the baseball out of the pool.

3. Tyler **hit** the floor after we slipped on Jello.

4. Will Alex **go** to the water ride before he leaves?

5. On Saturday, Shakespeare **swims** before dark.

6. Kelsey **is** an actor at Grammar World.

7. Kelly **was** the new water shooter.

8. The best day for the boat race **will be** Saturday.

9. Cory **seemed** sure that he would be the first one on the bus to Grammar World.

10. They **are** athletic.

11. Kathy wished she **could** attend the dance at Grammar World.

12. Aaron **shall** marry the water park princess.

13. Shawn **should** drive the bus to the field trip.

14. Will Portia **have** enough money to swim all day long?

15. Because she has a cold, Molly **will** not get to go to the evening swimming performance.

16. Peter **quickly** ran down the hill to reach the pool.

17. Dillon knew **immediately** that he was going to have a great time.

18. **Suddenly**, Lindsey was chilled to the bone.

19. Kelsey and Devin **slowly** decided that they would stay until the fireworks show ended.

20. Shakespeare *sadly* waved good-bye to all the children as they left Grammar World.

21. *Action verb:* The principal **called** Portia into her office.

22. *Linking verb:* Tracy **is** at the water park.

23. *Helping verb:* Lois **will** join the swim team.

24. *Adverb:* *Silently*, Tom watched the dolphin show with his friend.

Answers to Let's Try It! Set #19
page 78

1. *2 (past tense)* Kathy **decided** to swim down the water tunnel on her stomach.

2. *3 (future tense)* Lois **will jump** into the icy-cold pool of blue water.

3. *1 (present tense)* Shakespeare **is watching** all the action from the side of the pool.

4. *3 (future tense)* Riley **will return** to Grammar World as soon as his parents let him.

5. *2 (past tense)* Dillon **decided** to buy a new swim suit for the class trip.

6. *2 (past tense)* The entire football team **crowded** into the baby pool with Shakespeare.

7. *1 (present tense)* Shakespeare **is** on a surfboard.

8. *2 (past tense)* On Saturday, the pools **were drained** in order to clean them.

9. *2 (past tense)* Tom and Devin **were competing** against each other to see who could make the biggest splash.

10. *2 (past tense)* Tom **won**.

11. **Future:** Scooter **will walk** to school tomorrow.

12. **Past:** Cory **walked** to school yesterday.

13. **Present:** Tyler **is walking** to school today.

14. **Future:** Karry **will splash** in the pool tomorrow.

15. **Past:** Joe **splashed** in the pool yesterday.

16. **Present:** Tracy **is splashing** in the pool today.

17. **Future:** Tracy **will slide** down the water tunnel tomorrow.

18. **Past**: Kelly **slid** down the water tunnel yesterday.

19. **Present**: Shakespeare **is sliding** down the water tunnel today.

Answers to Let's Try It! Set # 20
page 81

1. Lauren and Scott **write** about the water park in their journals.

2. Adrianna **watches** the swimmers jump into the waterfall.

3. Molly always **wishes** upon a star at the fireworks show.

4. Joe **waxes** his surfboard every day.

5. Tyler **is buying** cool Hawaiian swimming trunks for the trip.

6. Peter **is taking** a good book to read because he has to stay out of the sun.

7. The entire class **is swimming** at night under the strobe lights.

8. Cory **rides** a wave.

9. Today, Scooter **races** to be the first in line.

10. Now I see how much fun we **are having**.

Answers to Verb Treasure Hunt
page 82

The water park <u>was</u> busy, busy, busy one hot and steamy August day. Everyone <u>had</u> the same idea of <u>visiting</u> Grammar World and <u>cooling</u> off at the refreshing water park. Children and adults alike <u>were swooshing</u> and <u>splashing</u> and <u>having</u> a grand old time.

Suddenly, a gigantic whirlpool <u>formed</u> and water <u>began</u> to <u>spin</u> and <u>swirl</u> like a tornado. What <u>could be causing</u> this? <u>Was</u> it a faulty drain? Maybe it <u>was</u> a weird windstorm of some sort. Everyone <u>tried</u> to get out of the water, but the current <u>was</u> too strong.

Answers to Let's Hit the Target!
Set # 3 *page 85*

1. linking verb (were)
2. action verb (loved)
3. helping verb (had)
4. past tense (watched)
5. past tense (decided)
6. helping verb (could)
7. past tense (were tired)
8. linking verb (is)
9. present tense (am)
10. adverb (quickly)

CHAPTER IV

Answers to Let's Try It! Set # 21
page 93

1. <u>On his way</u> <u>to the bus</u>, Aaron saw his friend.
2. The whistle used <u>at the water show</u> was hollow <u>in the middle</u>.
3. The trainer startled the animals when he jumped <u>into the pool</u>.
4. <u>After a day's rest</u>, Lauren went <u>on the field trip</u> <u>with her class</u>.
5. Peter's sunglasses fell <u>behind the bleachers</u> <u>at the dolphin show</u>.
6. <u>On Thursday</u>, the entire school took the bus <u>to Grammar World</u>.
7. <u>In a flash</u>, Cory was ready to line up and leave <u>with the group</u>.

8. Tyler smiled when he saw Shakespeare riding <u>on a dolphin</u>.

Answers to Prepositional Phrase Treasure Hunt *page 94*

Tragedy at Grammar World

Tragedy has struck Grammar World! Everyone is ⬚in a tizzy⬚!

The new baby tiger, Stripes, is missing. He was last seen ⬚with his mother⬚ ⬚during the noon feeding time.⬚

The keeper remembers seeing Stripes taking a snooze nestled snugly ⬚against his mother.⬚

Oh where, oh where, could Stripes have gone?

Answers to Let's Try It! Set #22 *page 97*

1. <u>Although</u> it was a cloudy day, the fifth-graders were excited about visiting Grammar World.

2. The bus was very crowded, <u>so</u> three students had to sit in each seat.

3. "We're getting as smooshed <u>as</u> pancakes!" yelled Riley <u>and</u> Jennifer.

4. "Please be patient <u>because</u> we are almost there," replied Mrs. Fewell.

5. Finally they arrived at the parking lot <u>and</u> were relieved that the cramped journey was almost over.

6. The students wanted to get off the bus, <u>but</u> Mrs. Fewell reminded them that they had to wait patiently for their turn.

7. Joe <u>and</u> Molly knew <u>that</u> they would be first in line <u>unless</u> Mrs. Fewell said otherwise.

8. They were all excited; <u>yet</u>, they were also packed in like sardines.

9. Finally, Mrs. Fewell gave the signal, <u>and</u> they tumbled off the bus like potatoes falling out of a bag.

10. <u>Because</u> the weather is warm today, I will be able to swim with the dolphins <u>and</u> the whales.

11. I would love to go to the water show with you, <u>but</u> I have already made other plans.

12. We will never visit the water park again <u>unless</u> you agree to go with us.

13. On the Fourth of July, Grammar World is always crowded <u>and</u> noisy.

Answers to Conjunction Treasure Hunt *page 98*

One steamy August day, herds of people made their way into Grammar World. It seemed <u>as if</u> everyone wanted to keep cool, <u>and</u> what better way to do so <u>than</u> by visiting the refreshing water park?

Within minutes after arriving at Grammar World, children <u>and</u> adults alike were splashing in the pool. Everyone was having a grand old time.

Suddenly, a gigantic whirlpool formed in the pool. The water began to swirl <u>and</u> spin like a tornado. What could be causing this? Was it a faulty drain <u>or</u> a strange windstorm of some sort? Everyone tried to get out of the water, <u>but</u> the current was too strong.

Answers to Let's Try It! Set # 23 *page 102*

1. "(Aha!) I have found the missing dolphin whistle," commented Shakespeare.

2. As Portia opened the kettle of dolphin fish treats, she exclaimed, "(Phew!)"

3. "(My goodness,)" remarked the chaperone as the class walked into the dolphin show.

4. When the show began Casey yelled, "(Hooray!)"

5. Karry exclaimed, "(Rats!) I cannot find a seat at the dolphin show."

Answers to Interjection Treasure Hunt *page 103*

"<u>Hey! Help!</u>" shouted the riders when the Ferris wheel broke down and came to a complete stop.

"<u>Oh, No!</u>" sobbed one rider. "<u>Eeeeeek!</u>"

"Get this ride going!" the others yelled. "<u>Now!</u>"

Suddenly, a child at the very top of the Ferris wheel crawled out of his seat and began to climb down the stalled ride. "<u>Ouch</u>," he exclaimed when one of his fingers scraped a ragged corner of the ride.

"<u>Help!</u> My baby has escaped!" his mother screamed frantically.

"<u>Mad rats!</u> This is certainly a dilemma," thought the operator of the Ferris wheel.

Answers to Let's Try It! Set # 24
page 105

1. <u>Yippee!</u> The seal just kissed me on my hand.

2. <u>Gee</u>, this is a breezy day for a trip to the water park.

3. <u>My goodness</u>, I never knew that penguins could be so funny.

4. <u>Wow!</u>

5. Tom exclaimed as he stepped on the gum, "<u>Yuck!</u>"

6. After the dolphin show the entire audience yelled, "<u>Bravo!</u>"

Answers to Let's Try It— Supersized! Set #25 *page 105*

1. The turtle was hiding <u>under</u> the rock.

2. Please go <u>around</u> the Water Show Building and meet me <u>at</u> the New Wave Aquarium.

3. We will go home <u>after</u> the last dolphin show.

4. You may sit <u>by</u> Aaron <u>on</u> the bus.

5. Your backpack is <u>under</u> the seat <u>of</u> the bus.

6. Joe wanted to pat the penguin on its head.

7. During the night, the trainer fed the animals.

8. Our class cheered when we were chosen to see the water show under the bridge.

9. Shakespeare sat under the diving board at the dolphin show.

10. Alex (and) Casey were picked to feed fish to the polar bears (and) penguins.

11. The sleepy students arrived home from the field trip (and) went straight to bed.

12. Josh (and) Christine couldn't wait to get to the park (because) they had front-row seats at the water show.

13. I want to snack on (either) popcorn (or) peanuts at the show.

14. [Good grief!] I am soaked from being splashed by the whale.

15. [Well,] I knew we would have a fabulous time.

16. [Cool beans!] The rides at Grammar World are out of this world.

17. The crowd screamed, ["Stop!"]

Answers to Let's Try It (Mixed Review)! Set # 26 *page 107*

1. <u>After</u> the water show, Kelsey got the chance to pet a dolphin <u>in</u> the tank.

2. He climbed <u>up</u> the stairs and ran quickly <u>to</u> the tank.

3. A huge smile appeared <u>on</u> his face as he touched the dolphin's smooth skin.

4. <u>On</u> Saturday, Peter traveled <u>with</u> the band <u>to</u> Grammar World .

5. [After the field trip,] Lauren skipped [to the bus,] fell

[on the stairs,] and skinned the top [of her knee.]

6. Her teacher found a special Scooby Doo Band-Aid to put [on her scraped knee.]

7. Lauren wrote a thank-you note [to her teacher.]

8. Whether you're [at school] or [on a field trip,] it's nice to have a caring teacher.

Draw <u>two lines</u> under each conjunction and <u>a dashed line</u> under each interjection<u>.</u>

9. <u>"Yikes!"</u> Devin yelled, <u>when</u> the water splashed out of the tank during the dolphin show.

10. Tim <u>and</u> Todd were so excited at the dolphin show <u>that</u> they screamed <u>"Whoopee"</u> after every trick.

Answers to Let's Hit the Target! Set #4 *page 114*

1. conjunction (and)

2. preposition (through)

3. interjection (Wow!)

4. prepositional phrase (through a giant hoop)

5. prepositional phrase (of the pool)

6. interjection (Ahhh!)

7. interjection (Bravo!)

CHAPTER V

Answers to Let's Hit the Target! Set #5 *page 128*

1. a period
2. a capital letter
3. quotation marks
4. a period
5. a question mark
6. a capital letter
7. an apostrophe

CHAPTER VI

Answers to Let's Hit the Target! Set #6 *page 136*

1. past tense (had closed)
2. article (The)
3. prepositional phrase (at the station)
4. adverb (quietly)
5. subject (The trainers)
6. conjunction (and)
7. adjective (blue)
8. article (A)
9. past tense (moaned)
10. subject (It)
11. linking verb (was)
12. adjective (dark)
13. interjection (Good grief!)

INDEX